GOD LOVES CHILDREN

Take Home!

MIRIAM HELPED (EXODUS 2:1-10)

Aim
To help the children understand that children can help in families.

Bible verses
Miriam helped look after her baby brother. (Exodus 2:4)
Children, obey your parents. (Ephesians 6:1)
We are helpers. (2 Corinthians 1:24)

The story
Miriam helped take care of her baby brother. He was growing fast. One day Mother said, 'The king does not want the baby boys to live. Our baby is getting too big for us to hide him. We must find a way to keep him safe.'

Mother made a basket for the baby. She put the baby in the basket. Mother and Miriam went down to the river. They put the basket in the tall grass by the edge of the water. 'Miriam, you stay here,' said Mother. 'Watch to see that our baby is safe.'

The king's daughter, who was the princess, came down to the river. She saw the basket floating in the water and heard the baby crying. She told one of her helpers to bring the basket to her. When she saw the baby boy in the basket she said, 'This is a lovely baby. I would like him to be my son.'

Miriam ran to the princess. 'Would you like me to find someone to look after this baby for you?' she asked. 'Yes, please,' said the princess. Miriam ran to get her mother.

The princess said, 'Please will you look after this baby for me until he is old enough to come and live with me at the palace. I will pay you to take care of him.' Mother was very happy to have her baby back. Now he would be safe. She took him home. Miriam had helped look after her baby brother. She had helped keep him safe.

When Miriam's brother went to live at the palace the princess named him Moses.

Activity suggestions

Look at pictures of families with babies
Look through magazines or catalogues to find pictures of families with babies, or look at photos of your own family. Show the pictures to your baby and talk about how babies are looked after in families. Tell your baby about Miriam and Moses. An older under five may want to cut pictures out and glue them to make a collage. Or they may want to draw their own picture of Miriam and Moses.

Finger-paint with shaving foam
A suitably protected table or worktop is ideal for this, or you can use a tray or baking sheet. Cover your child's clothes well. Squirt a blob of shaving foam onto your working surface and let your child 'finger-paint' with the foam. When it runs out, squirt some more. This is a messy activity, but great fun. Some children will dive straight in with both hands. Others may be more cautious and use only one finger! As you supervise the children in this activity, tell them about Miriam and Moses.

BIBLE STUFF

GOD LOVES CHILDREN — WEEK 1

Take Home!

MIRIAM HELPED (EXODUS 2:1-10)

Aim
To help the children understand that children can help in families.

Bible verses
Miriam helped look after her baby brother. (Exodus 2:4)
Children, obey your parents. (Ephesians 6:1)
We are helpers. (2 Corinthians 1:24)

The story
Miriam helped take care of her baby brother. He was growing fast. One day Mother said, 'The king does not want the baby boys to live. Our baby is getting too big for us to hide him. We must find a way to keep him safe.'

Mother made a basket for the baby. She put the baby in the basket. Mother and Miriam went down to the river. They put the basket in the tall grass by the edge of the water. 'Miriam, you stay here,' said Mother. 'Watch to see that our baby is safe.'

The king's daughter, who was the princess, came down to the river. She saw the basket floating in the water and heard the baby crying. She told one of her helpers to bring the basket to her. When she saw the baby boy in the basket she said, 'This is a lovely baby. I would like him to be my son.'

Miriam ran to the princess. 'Would you like me to find someone to look after this baby for you?' she asked. 'Yes, please,' said the princess. Miriam ran to get her mother.

The princess said, 'Please will you look after this baby for me until he is old enough to come and live with me at the palace. I will pay you to take care of him.' Mother was very happy to have her baby back. Now he would be safe. She took him home. Miriam had helped look after her baby brother. She had helped keep him safe.

When Miriam's brother went to live at the palace the princess named him Moses.

Activity suggestions

Look at pictures of families with babies
Look through magazines or catalogues to find pictures of families with babies, or look at photos of your own family. Show the pictures to your baby and talk about how babies are looked after in families. Tell your baby about Miriam and Moses. An older under five may want to cut pictures out and glue them to make a collage. Or they may want to draw their own picture of Miriam and Moses.

Finger-paint with shaving foam
A suitably protected table or worktop is ideal for this, or you can use a tray or baking sheet. Cover your child's clothes well. Squirt a blob of shaving foam onto your working surface and let your child 'finger-paint' with the foam. When it runs out, squirt some more. This is a messy activity, but great fun. Some children will dive straight in with both hands. Others may be more cautious and use only one finger! As you supervise the children in this activity, tell them about Miriam and Moses.

GOD LOVES CHILDREN — WEEK 1

Take Home!

MIRIAM HELPED (EXODUS 2:1-10)

Aim
To help the children understand that children can help in families.

Bible verses
Miriam helped look after her baby brother. (Exodus 2:4)
Children, obey your parents. (Ephesians 6:1)
We are helpers. (2 Corinthians 1:24)

The story
Miriam helped take care of her baby brother. He was growing fast. One day Mother said, 'The king does not want the baby boys to live. Our baby is getting too big for us to hide him. We must find a way to keep him safe.'

Mother made a basket for the baby. She put the baby in the basket. Mother and Miriam went down to the river. They put the basket in the tall grass by the edge of the water. 'Miriam, you stay here,' said Mother. 'Watch to see that our baby is safe.'

The king's daughter, who was the princess, came down to the river. She saw the basket floating in the water and heard the baby crying. She told one of her helpers to bring the basket to her. When she saw the baby boy in the basket she said, 'This is a lovely baby. I would like him to be my son.'

Miriam ran to the princess. 'Would you like me to find someone to look after this baby for you?' she asked. 'Yes, please,' said the princess. Miriam ran to get her mother.

The princess said, 'Please will you look after this baby for me until he is old enough to come and live with me at the palace. I will pay you to take care of him.' Mother was very happy to have her baby back. Now he would be safe. She took him home. Miriam had helped look after her baby brother. She had helped keep him safe.

When Miriam's brother went to live at the palace the princess named him Moses.

Activity suggestions

Look at pictures of families with babies
Look through magazines or catalogues to find pictures of families with babies, or look at photos of your own family. Show the pictures to your baby and talk about how babies are looked after in families. Tell your baby about Miriam and Moses. An older under five may want to cut pictures out and glue them to make a collage. Or they may want to draw their own picture of Miriam and Moses.

Finger-paint with shaving foam
A suitably protected table or worktop is ideal for this, or you can use a tray or baking sheet. Cover your child's clothes well. Squirt a blob of shaving foam onto your working surface and let your child 'finger-paint' with the foam. When it runs out, squirt some more. This is a messy activity, but great fun. Some children will dive straight in with both hands. Others may be more cautious and use only one finger! As you supervise the children in this activity, tell them about Miriam and Moses.

GOD LOVES CHILDREN — WEEK 1

Take Home!

MIRIAM HELPED (EXODUS 2:1-10)

Aim
To help the children understand that children can help in families.

Bible verses
Miriam helped look after her baby brother. (Exodus 2:4)
Children, obey your parents. (Ephesians 6:1)
We are helpers. (2 Corinthians 1:24)

The story
Miriam helped take care of her baby brother. He was growing fast. One day Mother said, 'The king does not want the baby boys to live. Our baby is getting too big for us to hide him. We must find a way to keep him safe.'

Mother made a basket for the baby. She put the baby in the basket. Mother and Miriam went down to the river. They put the basket in the tall grass by the edge of the water. 'Miriam, you stay here,' said Mother. 'Watch to see that our baby is safe.'

The king's daughter, who was the princess, came down to the river. She saw the basket floating in the water and heard the baby crying. She told one of her helpers to bring the basket to her. When she saw the baby boy in the basket she said, 'This is a lovely baby. I would like him to be my son.'

Miriam ran to the princess. 'Would you like me to find someone to look after this baby for you?' she asked. 'Yes, please,' said the princess. Miriam ran to get her mother.

The princess said, 'Please will you look after this baby for me until he is old enough to come and live with me at the palace. I will pay you to take care of him.' Mother was very happy to have her baby back. Now he would be safe. She took him home. Miriam had helped look after her baby brother. She had helped keep him safe.

When Miriam's brother went to live at the palace the princess named him Moses.

Activity suggestions

Look at pictures of families with babies
Look through magazines or catalogues to find pictures of families with babies, or look at photos of your own family. Show the pictures to your baby and talk about how babies are looked after in families. Tell your baby about Miriam and Moses. An older under five may want to cut pictures out and glue them to make a collage. Or they may want to draw their own picture of Miriam and Moses.

Finger-paint with shaving foam
A suitably protected table or worktop is ideal for this, or you can use a tray or baking sheet. Cover your child's clothes well. Squirt a blob of shaving foam onto your working surface and let your child 'finger-paint' with the foam. When it runs out, squirt some more. This is a messy activity, but great fun. Some children will dive straight in with both hands. Others may be more cautious and use only one finger! As you supervise the children in this activity, tell them about Miriam and Moses.

GOD LOVES CHILDREN — WEEK 1

Take Home!

MIRIAM HELPED (EXODUS 2:1-10)

Aim
To help the children understand that children can help in families.

Bible verses
Miriam helped look after her baby brother. (Exodus 2:4)
Children, obey your parents. (Ephesians 6:1)
We are helpers. (2 Corinthians 1:24)

The story
Miriam helped take care of her baby brother. He was growing fast. One day Mother said, 'The king does not want the baby boys to live. Our baby is getting too big for us to hide him. We must find a way to keep him safe.'

Mother made a basket for the baby. She put the baby in the basket. Mother and Miriam went down to the river. They put the basket in the tall grass by the edge of the water. 'Miriam, you stay here,' said Mother. 'Watch to see that our baby is safe.'

The king's daughter, who was the princess, came down to the river. She saw the basket floating in the water and heard the baby crying. She told one of her helpers to bring the basket to her. When she saw the baby boy in the basket she said, 'This is a lovely baby. I would like him to be my son.'

Miriam ran to the princess. 'Would you like me to find someone to look after this baby for you?' she asked. 'Yes, please,' said the princess. Miriam ran to get her mother.

The princess said, 'Please will you look after this baby for me until he is old enough to come and live with me at the palace. I will pay you to take care of him.' Mother was very happy to have her baby back. Now he would be safe. She took him home. Miriam had helped look after her baby brother. She had helped keep him safe.

When Miriam's brother went to live at the palace the princess named him Moses.

Activity suggestions

Look at pictures of families with babies
Look through magazines or catalogues to find pictures of families with babies, or look at photos of your own family. Show the pictures to your baby and talk about how babies are looked after in families. Tell your baby about Miriam and Moses. An older under five may want to cut pictures out and glue them to make a collage. Or they may want to draw their own picture of Miriam and Moses.

Finger-paint with shaving foam
A suitably protected table or worktop is ideal for this, or you can use a tray or baking sheet. Cover your child's clothes well. Squirt a blob of shaving foam onto your working surface and let your child 'finger-paint' with the foam. When it runs out, squirt some more. This is a messy activity, but great fun. Some children will dive straight in with both hands. Others may be more cautious and use only one finger! As you supervise the children in this activity, tell them about Miriam and Moses.

GOD LOVES CHILDREN — WEEK 1

Take Home!

MIRIAM HELPED (EXODUS 2:1-10)

Aim
To help the children understand that children can help in families.

Bible verses
Miriam helped look after her baby brother. (Exodus 2:4)
Children, obey your parents. (Ephesians 6:1)
We are helpers. (2 Corinthians 1:24)

The story
Miriam helped take care of her baby brother. He was growing fast. One day Mother said, 'The king does not want the baby boys to live. Our baby is getting too big for us to hide him. We must find a way to keep him safe.'

Mother made a basket for the baby. She put the baby in the basket. Mother and Miriam went down to the river. They put the basket in the tall grass by the edge of the water. 'Miriam, you stay here,' said Mother. 'Watch to see that our baby is safe.'

The king's daughter, who was the princess, came down to the river. She saw the basket floating in the water and heard the baby crying. She told one of her helpers to bring the basket to her. When she saw the baby boy in the basket she said, 'This is a lovely baby. I would like him to be my son.'

Miriam ran to the princess. 'Would you like me to find someone to look after this baby for you?' she asked. 'Yes, please,' said the princess. Miriam ran to get her mother.

The princess said, 'Please will you look after this baby for me until he is old enough to come and live with me at the palace. I will pay you to take care of him.' Mother was very happy to have her baby back. Now he would be safe. She took him home. Miriam had helped look after her baby brother. She had helped keep him safe.

When Miriam's brother went to live at the palace the princess named him Moses.

Activity suggestions

Look at pictures of families with babies
Look through magazines or catalogues to find pictures of families with babies, or look at photos of your own family. Show the pictures to your baby and talk about how babies are looked after in families. Tell your baby about Miriam and Moses. An older under five may want to cut pictures out and glue them to make a collage. Or they may want to draw their own picture of Miriam and Moses.

Finger-paint with shaving foam
A suitably protected table or worktop is ideal for this, or you can use a tray or baking sheet. Cover your child's clothes well. Squirt a blob of shaving foam onto your working surface and let your child 'finger-paint' with the foam. When it runs out, squirt some more. This is a messy activity, but great fun. Some children will dive straight in with both hands. Others may be more cautious and use only one finger! As you supervise the children in this activity, tell them about Miriam and Moses.

GOD LOVES CHILDREN — WEEK 1

Take Home!

MIRIAM HELPED (EXODUS 2:1-10)

Aim
To help the children understand that children can help in families.

Bible verses
Miriam helped look after her baby brother. (Exodus 2:4)
Children, obey your parents. (Ephesians 6:1)
We are helpers. (2 Corinthians 1:24)

The story
Miriam helped take care of her baby brother. He was growing fast. One day Mother said, 'The king does not want the baby boys to live. Our baby is getting too big for us to hide him. We must find a way to keep him safe.'

Mother made a basket for the baby. She put the baby in the basket. Mother and Miriam went down to the river. They put the basket in the tall grass by the edge of the water. 'Miriam, you stay here,' said Mother. 'Watch to see that our baby is safe.'

The king's daughter, who was the princess, came down to the river. She saw the basket floating in the water and heard the baby crying. She told one of her helpers to bring the basket to her. When she saw the baby boy in the basket she said, 'This is a lovely baby. I would like him to be my son.'

Miriam ran to the princess. 'Would you like me to find someone to look after this baby for you?' she asked. 'Yes, please,' said the princess. Miriam ran to get her mother.

The princess said, 'Please will you look after this baby for me until he is old enough to come and live with me at the palace. I will pay you to take care of him.' Mother was very happy to have her baby back. Now he would be safe. She took him home. Miriam had helped look after her baby brother. She had helped keep him safe.

When Miriam's brother went to live at the palace the princess named him Moses.

Activity suggestions

Look at pictures of families with babies
Look through magazines or catalogues to find pictures of families with babies, or look at photos of your own family. Show the pictures to your baby and talk about how babies are looked after in families. Tell your baby about Miriam and Moses. An older under five may want to cut pictures out and glue them to make a collage. Or they may want to draw their own picture of Miriam and Moses.

Finger-paint with shaving foam
A suitably protected table or worktop is ideal for this, or you can use a tray or baking sheet. Cover your child's clothes well. Squirt a blob of shaving foam onto your working surface and let your child 'finger-paint' with the foam. When it runs out, squirt some more. This is a messy activity, but great fun. Some children will dive straight in with both hands. Others may be more cautious and use only one finger! As you supervise the children in this activity, tell them about Miriam and Moses.

Bible Stuff

Spiritual Teaching for
Under Fives that's Fun

God Loves Children
Jesus is our Friend

Janet Gaukroger

Contents

God loves Children

Week 1	**Miriam Helped**	4
Week 2	**Samuel Loved God**	9
Week 3	**Naaman's Slave Girl**	14
Week 4	**Jesus and the Children**	19

Jesus is our friend

Week 1	**Jesus Feeds the People**	24
Week 2	**Jesus Heals a Blind Man**	29
Week 3	**Jesus Teaches the People**	34
Week 4	**People Sing to Jesus**	39
Week 5	**Friends See Jesus**	44

Introduction

Welcome to *Bible Stuff* – an activity-based curriculum designed to help us communicate spiritual truth to children from birth to age five.

Basic beliefs

There's no doubt that children take in a massive amount of information in the first five years of their lives. Many significant attitudes and habits are formed which will last a lifetime. It is so important that we pass on the Christian faith to our children from the very beginning. We have the opportunity to give them a heritage of spiritual strength. *Bible Stuff* is one attempt to help us make the most of that opportunity by combining a number of factors to produce an effective programme. The programme's four basic beliefs are as follows.

1. Communicating Biblical truth is very important

Bible Stuff is committed to the truth and accuracy of the Bible as God's Word, living and active in today's world. Teaching it to the next generation is a serious responsibility.

2. Teaching in ways that under fives can understand is crucial

We have not effectively taught the Bible if the recipients of our teaching have not learned. We must, therefore, understand where under fives are in their physical, mental, spiritual and emotional development so that we can teach in ways they will relate to.

3. Children learn through play

Recognizing that play is the child's work means choosing activities that are fun, but that are also part of the development process.

4. Children are all different

Providing a variety of activities simultaneously allows a child to express his or her own personality by choosing what to be involved in. (*Bible Stuff* does not recommend everybody doing the same thing at the same time. It recognizes that one child may be happy to play in the home corner for an entire session, and another child may need the stimulation of four or five different things in the same period of time.)

This curriculum has been tried and tested by the under fives teachers at Stopsley Baptist Church in Luton. I owe them a great deal for their loyalty and support over many years.

May God envision, encourage and empower us through his Holy Spirit as we 'tell the next generation the praiseworthy deeds of the Lord' (Psalm 78:4).

How to use this book

Bible Stuff contains two teaching units, one of four weeks and one of five. The story and activities for each week are completely self-contained, though spending four or five weeks on the same theme reinforces the teaching. For each session you will find:

 Preparation

This includes Bible background or a meditation for teachers – we need to feed on God's word ourselves in order to teach effectively.

 Story Time

This section includes a short selection of Bible verses related to the theme of the session. They are paraphrased in language under fives can understand. Use them throughout the session as you talk to and with the babies and children. The more they hear us saying 'The Bible says...', the more they will learn what a special book it is.

Teaching Activities

These are divided into activities for babies, toddlers, 2s – 3s and 3s – 5s. Again, if your class combines ages, choose an activity from each age group. You will find that some of them overlap.

 Group Time

There are separate suggestions for 2s – 3s and 3s – 5s. If you are working with babies and toddlers, sitting them all down at once to hear the story is rarely a possibility. Don't worry – you can be telling them parts of the story all through the session. In fact, you can do that with all under fives, so that when they hear the story in group time, it will have a familiar ring.

Take Home!

Each session ends with a photocopiable take-home paper. This is to give to parents or carers and is designed so that they can follow up the teaching at home. It gives the story and Bible verses, then two or three suggestions for home-based activities, at least one of which is suitable for babies. You may need to give some explanation and encouragement to the parents / carers to help them make the most of the take-home sheet.

Planning

Start by reading through the whole unit: some activities require the collection of various items in advance. Also, teachers can share responsibility for bringing any necessary equipment. Some activities are suggested for more than one age group, so if you have more than one class of under fives, co-ordination between groups will help all concerned.

Setting up

If possible, try to have the room ready when children arrive. This creates a more relaxed atmosphere. You do not need a lot of fancy equipment or expensive toys. For under fives, bricks, a simple home corner, puzzles and books should be available at every session. They give a sense of continuity and are also the most-used items for this age group. Don't put out all of your equipment each time you meet. Using the activities suggested for each week adds variety. Look through them to make a basic equipment list.

Group time

Group time comes at the end of each session and is an important part of the teaching / learning process, but it is not the only part. It's to be hoped that teaching will be going on throughout the session in the various activities. Group time should be between five and ten minutes long, depending on the age and maturity level of the children. Its components are conversation, singing, prayer, telling the Bible story and sometimes a 'game' or 'activity'. The order of these components can vary from session to session. Try to choose the moment when the children are most settled to tell the story. Sometimes some of the children may want to pray, sometimes only a teacher will pray. You may find that you need to sing four or five songs to settle children, and another time it will only take one. Try to have several ideas ready for group time, but remain flexible.

Health and safety

Never leave children unsupervised when using sand, water and dough. If necessary, put these items out of reach until you can come back to them. If you are in any doubt about mess, cover the children's clothing with aprons. If you are not sure about safety guidelines, ask someone who is. Check with your local social services office, get information from your local library or make contact with the person responsible for health and safety in your church building.

> **Resources**
> The following books offer detailed help and information:
> *Sharing Jesus with Under Fives*, Janet Gaukroger, Crossway Books
> *Children in Crèches and Toddler Groups*, Ann Croft, CPAS

God Loves Children   Week 1

MIRIAM HELPED (EXODUS 2:1-10)

Aim To help the children understand that children can help in families.

Preparation

The order from Pharaoh was for the murder of all boys born to Hebrew women. When Moses was born, his mother Jochebed could not bear to let him go. She managed to hide him for three months. She saw that he was a beautiful baby. Some scholars believe that she may have had an inkling that he was anointed by God, somehow linked to the promise of God for the Hebrews.

Jochebed knew you can't hide a baby for ever, so she devised a plan which would need the help of her daughter Miriam. It's possible that Miriam may have been following her mother's instructions when she ran to Pharaoh's daughter and offered to fetch a nurse for the baby. Or she may have been a very astute girl, acting on her own quick thinking. Whichever is true, Miriam was vital to Moses' survival and early instruction in a Hebrew home. If Jochebed had been hiding near the river, it would have been obvious that the baby was hers. But Miriam was mistaken for a girl who just happened to be playing by the river and who saw what happened.

It is obvious to us as adults that God used a young girl to further his purposes. We may not be able to convey this to under fives. But what we can help them to understand is that children can be helpers in families. They can see that Miriam helped to look after her baby brother as well as her mother. Let's teach this as a foundation for understanding later on that children are important in the purposes of God, and that he wants to use them in his kingdom.

Here are two possibilities of what God might want to say to us through this story:

Miriam's role was small but strategic. She received no praise, but God worked out his purposes through her. What we do for God may not seem glamorous or even important - only eternity will show what part our faithfulness plays in God's kingdom.

God had anointed Moses from birth - a common biblical concept. Though his mother's influence lasted only a few years, it was crucial: she taught him to know the one true God. As we teach young children week by week to know God, we are building significant foundations for their lives. Our faithfulness to this task may result in one of them accomplishing great things for the King.

The word of God is living and active. He longs to speak to us through it every time we read it. Try to take a few minutes this week to read this story again, and ask God what he wants to say to you through it. And be encouraged - God loves the children we teach. He is already working in their lives. And we have the privilege of being part of that work.

'Lord, please help me to be more aware of and more sensitive to the children in my church. Help me to show them that you love and value them. I pray that I may communicate to the children their worth in your eyes - in the things I teach them and in all that I do at church. Amen.'

Story Time

Bible verses
Miriam helped look after her baby brother. (Exodus 2:4)
Children, obey your parents. (Ephesians 6:1)
We are helpers. (2 Corinthians 1:24)

BIBLE STUFF   God Loves Children/Jesus is our Friend   4

Week 1

Birth - 2s

Miriam helped take care of her baby brother. He was growing fast.

One day Mother said, 'The king does not want the baby boys to live. We must find a way to keep our baby safe.'

Mother made a basket for the baby. She put the baby in the basket. Mother and Miriam took the basket to the edge of the river. They put the basket in the tall grass at the edge of the water.

Mother said to Miriam, 'You stay here and watch the baby.'

Miriam did what her mother told her.

The princess came to the river. She saw the baby in the basket. She said, 'This is a lovely baby. I would like him to be my son.'

Miriam ran to the princess and said, 'Would you like me to find someone to look after this baby for you?'

'Yes, please,' said the princess.

Miriam ran to get her mother. The princess said, 'Please look after this baby for me until he is old enough to live with me at the palace.'

Mother was happy to have her baby back safely with her. Miriam had helped to look after her baby brother.

Later on, the princess named the baby Moses.

3s - 5s

Miriam helped take care of her baby brother. He was growing fast. One day Mother said, 'The king does not want the baby boys to live. Our baby is getting too big for us to hide him. We must find a way to keep him safe.'

Mother made a basket for the baby. She put the baby in the basket. Mother and Miriam went down to the river. They put the basket in the tall grass by the edge of the water. 'Miriam, you stay here,' said Mother. 'Watch to see that our baby is safe.'

The king's daughter, who was the princess, came down to the river. She saw the basket floating in the water and heard the baby crying. She told one of her helpers to bring the basket to her. When she saw the baby boy in the basket she said, 'This is a lovely baby. I would like him to be my son.'

Miriam ran to the princess. 'Would you like me to find someone to look after this baby for you?' she asked. 'Yes, please,' said the princess. Miriam ran to get her mother.

The princess said, 'Please will you look after this baby for me until he is old enough to come and live with me at the palace. I will pay you to take care of him.' Mother was very happy to have her baby back. Now he would be safe. She took him home. Miriam had helped look after her baby brother. She had helped keep him safe.

When Miriam's brother went to live at the palace the princess named him Moses.

Teaching Activities

This unit on children will emphasize their value in God's kingdom. We believe this, but we don't always live it out in practice. Let's demonstrate the value we place on children in both the way we teach and in the way we behave to all the children in our church. It's easy to speak to adults and completely ignore children. Let's make them feel part of our church family by greeting them by name and taking time to talk to them.

BIBLE STUFF   God Loves Children/Jesus is our Friend

week 1

Babies

Look at pictures of families with babies Look in old magazines or catalogues to find four or five pictures of families with babies. Mount them individually, or put them together to make a book. As you show the pictures to the babies, tell them about Miriam helping to look after her baby brother. If the baby you are talking to has older siblings, talk about his or her own family.

Play with buckets and spades Provide several small plastic buckets and spades for babies to play with today. If you do not have any, it shouldn't be too hard to find a family that you can borrow some from. Give them a good scrub to ensure they are clean. Let babies use the buckets and spades as toys. They don't need sand. Some babies may have been or are going to the seaside for holidays. Talk to them about the beach. Thank God for happy times with families.

Finger-paint with lotion Provide a wipe-clean tray and some baby lotion, as well as tissues for wiping fingers. Squirt a small amount of lotion onto the tray and guide an older baby to put a finger or whole hand in the lotion and 'finger-paint' with it. Supervise carefully to ensure that babies do not swallow any lotion. Tell them some of today's Bible story. When they have finished, wipe off any excess lotion with tissues. Make sure that every baby feels loved and cared for, however they respond to any activity.

Toddlers

Use pictures of families with babies today. You may want to put them in a book and write an appropriate phrase on each page: 'Thank you, God for families'; 'Brothers and sisters can help'; 'Children can help their parents'.

Easel paint Cover the floor with newspaper and give out painting aprons. Provide large sheets of paper for children to paint at the easel. As a child paints, you may be able to share one or two of today's Bible verses. But don't worry if you don't say anything 'spiritual'. We teach as much by what we do as by what we say.

Care for a doll Bring a baby bottle, a bib, a nappy and a doll's buggy if you have access to one. Help the children pretend to care for the doll. If you do bring a buggy, they will need help in taking turns with it!

2s - 3s

Have a visit from a mother and baby Ask a mother (and father, if possible) with a fairly young baby to visit the children. They could show the children how they look after their baby. If they can arrange the timing right, they could give the baby a bottle. Some of the children may have a baby brother or sister, so talk about children helping to care for babies. Relate this to Miriam helping to look after her brother.

Put clothes on a washing line String up a short washing line at very low level. Bring a variety of items that children can lay over the line. Bring a few pegs, but most will be happy to lay clothes over the line. You may want to bring the clothes in a small washing basket. As you help children with this activity, talk about their families. Tell them about Miriam's family.

Finger-paint with shaving foam Bring a wipe-clean tray and some shaving foam; provide painting aprons. Squirt a small amount of foam onto the tray. Some children will go straight in with both hands, others may be hesitant or even decide they don't like it. The children should feel completely accepted whether they want to 'paint' or not. Try sprinkling some powder paint on the foam. When the child has finished making a pattern, press a piece of white paper onto the foam to make a print. It's advisable to practise this activity at home. Provide a bowl of soapy water for washing hands.

Week 1

Look at pictures of children playing and helping Search in old magazines and catalogues for pictures of children playing and helping at home. Spread the pictures out on the floor. Talk with the children about their own families. Some may have grandparents or child-minders who help look after them. Tell them about Miriam helping in her family.

3s - 5s

This age group will also enjoy a visit from a baby today. They will also enjoy putting clothes on a washing line.

Paint at the easel Use large sheets of paper. Provide painting aprons, chunky brushes and between two and four colours of paint. As children paint, tell them about Miriam, or share today's Bible verses with them.

Sand play Provide some beach toys for the sand today. Place one or two small buckets, spades and 'sand moulds' for the children to work with. You will need to add water to make the sand wet enough to hold a shape. Always supervise sand play very carefully. Provide aprons and soapy water for washing hands.

Group Time

2s - 3s

As children help to tidy the room for group time, sing a song about helping, with words such as 'I will be a helper' or 'It's time to put the toys away, who can be a helper?' While children are settling for group time, take time to thank individual children for being helpful, co-operative or for being thoughtful towards other children.

After you tell the story of Miriam, you may want to talk about ways the children can help. This is not always easy, because very young children can only help in limited ways. But it is good for them to begin to understand about helping. We want them to begin to see, also, that obeying their parents is a way of helping.

At the end, show the pictures of children and families that you were using during the session. Also, you could take turns throwing a beach ball or bean bag to each other.

3s - 5s

As with 2s and 3s, emphasize the theme of helping through songs and conversation. Sometimes children do not get much opportunity to help at home. Although it is good training to let children help, doing so can lengthen the task. Some parents find it hard to take the time to let children help. Let's try to find ways to let them help at church where we are not under the same pressure as parents in the home. At the end, you can roll or throw a beach ball with the children.

BIBLE STUFF   *God Loves Children/Jesus is our Friend*

GOD LOVES CHILDREN — WEEK 1

Take Home!

MIRIAM HELPED (EXODUS 2:1-10)

Aim
To help the children understand that children can help in families.

Bible verses
Miriam helped look after her baby brother. (Exodus 2:4)
Children, obey your parents. (Ephesians 6:1)
We are helpers. (2 Corinthians 1:24)

The story
Miriam helped take care of her baby brother. He was growing fast. One day Mother said, 'The king does not want the baby boys to live. Our baby is getting too big for us to hide him. We must find a way to keep him safe.'

Mother made a basket for the baby. She put the baby in the basket. Mother and Miriam went down to the river. They put the basket in the tall grass by the edge of the water. 'Miriam, you stay here,' said Mother. 'Watch to see that our baby is safe.'

The king's daughter, who was the princess, came down to the river. She saw the basket floating in the water and heard the baby crying. She told one of her helpers to bring the basket to her. When she saw the baby boy in the basket she said, 'This is a lovely baby. I would like him to be my son.'

Miriam ran to the princess. 'Would you like me to find someone to look after this baby for you?' she asked. 'Yes, please,' said the princess. Miriam ran to get her mother.

The princess said, 'Please will you look after this baby for me until he is old enough to come and live with me at the palace. I will pay you to take care of him.' Mother was very happy to have her baby back. Now he would be safe. She took him home. Miriam had helped look after her baby brother. She had helped keep him safe.

When Miriam's brother went to live at the palace the princess named him Moses.

Activity suggestions

Look at pictures of families with babies
Look through magazines or catalogues to find pictures of families with babies, or look at photos of your own family. Show the pictures to your baby and talk about how babies are looked after in families. Tell your baby about Miriam and Moses. An older under five may want to cut pictures out and glue them to make a collage. Or they may want to draw their own picture of Miriam and Moses.

Finger-paint with shaving foam
A suitably protected table or worktop is ideal for this, or you can use a tray or baking sheet. Cover your child's clothes well. Squirt a blob of shaving foam onto your working surface and let your child 'finger-paint' with the foam. When it runs out, squirt some more. This is a messy activity, but great fun. Some children will dive straight in with both hands. Others may be more cautious and use only one finger! As you supervise the children in this activity, tell them about Miriam and Moses.

BIBLE STUFF — God Loves Children/Jesus is our Friend

God Loves Children — Week 2

SAMUEL LOVED GOD (1 SAMUEL 3)

Aim To help the children understand that children can love God and can do things to help at church.

Preparation

If anyone ever doubted the significance of children in the kingdom of God, they need only read the story of young Samuel. Here is a case of God clearly having his hand on someone's life from the very beginning. In fact, even Samuel's birth required an act of God, for his mother Hannah was barren. Out of impossible circumstances, God worked to fulfil his purposes for Israel. Samuel may have been as young as some of the children we teach when he began his life of service to God!

We don't know how old Samuel was at the time of the events recorded in Chapter 3. He might have been as young as eight or nine or he could have been a teenager. He is referred to as 'the boy', which indicates someone who has not yet reached physical and mental maturity. It was at this point that Samuel first began to hear and respond clearly to the word of God. He had had no previous experience similar to the call he received from God in the night. The Bible tells us that direct words from God were rare in those days.

Despite his fear of having to tell Eli, Samuel responded faithfully to God's call. Poor Samuel! His first prophetic utterance was to proclaim judgement on the man who taught him to listen to God in the first place! He was probably thinking, 'God, couldn't you give this job to someone else?'

Samuel remained at the temple at Shiloh. He continued to serve Eli and he grew up in spiritual maturity. The people respected Samuel, even in his youth, as one who was in touch with God.

May it be our goal to pass on the faith clearly to the children we teach so that they will grow up learning to listen to God. Let's help them to understand from the beginning that they are part of God's family. God doesn't set a minimum age for his servants.

Let's ask God to show us how we can value the children in our church family more highly than we have done before. Wouldn't it be great to watch a generation of children grow up with the moving of God in their lives plain for all to see? They won't all be great prophets like Samuel. But it would be lovely to watch them grow in grace, fulfilling all their potential as men and women of God. This isn't a pipe dream. I believe that it is a vision which God longs to make a reality among us. We must pray and work to that end.

'Lord, I pray for each of the children that I teach. I pray that their experiences on Sunday at church will be a positive and important part of them growing up to love you and be open to you. Help me and others in the church to nurture the children lovingly and carefully in the faith. Amen.'

Story Time

Bible verses
Samuel helped Eli at church. (1 Samuel 3:1)
Samuel wanted to do the things that made God happy. (1 Samuel 2:26)
The people knew that Samuel loved God and that he helped at church. (1 Samuel 3:19,20)

Week 2

Birth - 2s

Samuel was a boy who loved God. Samuel helped Eli the teacher at church. He learned about God from teacher Eli.

One night Samuel heard someone call his name. He ran to Eli and said, 'Here I am. What do you need?' But Eli had not called Samuel. Eli said, 'I did not call you. Go back and lie down.'

Samuel heard someone call his name two more times and he went to teacher Eli. At last Eli knew that God was talking to Samuel. He told Samuel, 'Go back and lie down. When you hear your name called again, say, "I am listening, God. What do you want to say to me?"'

Samuel did what Eli said. He loved God and he wanted to do the things God wanted. As Samuel grew up he stayed at the church to help Eli. He learned more about God.

3s - 5s

Samuel was a boy who loved God. He helped Eli the teacher at church. Samuel learned about God from Eli.

One night Samuel heard someone call his name. He ran to Eli and said, 'Here I am. What do you need?' But Eli had not called Samuel. Eli said, 'I did not call you. Go back and lie down.'

Samuel went back to lie down. But he heard his name again. He went back to Eli, but it was not Eli who had called his name. Again, Samuel heard his name. This time when he went to Eli, the teacher knew that it was God talking to Samuel. Eli said, 'Go back and lie down. When you hear your name called again, say, "I am listening, God. What do you want to say to me?"'

Samuel did what Eli said. He loved God and wanted to do the things God wanted. As Samuel grew up, lots of people were his friends. They knew that he loved God and wanted to please God. Samuel stayed at the church to help Eli. As he grew up, he learned more about God.

Teaching Activities

Babies

Look at pictures of church buildings Find three or four pictures of different types of church buildings. Mount them on card or make them into a book. If possible include a picture of your own church building. As you show the pictures to babies, tell them about Samuel helping Eli at church. We can only guess at the exact nature of his chores: trimming the lamps, cleaning the various fittings, and making sure the doors and curtains were open and closed at the right time.

Play with dishes Borrow some toy dishes for babies to play with today - a few plates, some cups and a saucepan. Having something different to play with usually stimulates interest, even with babies. As they play, tell them about today's Bible verses.

Make a 'fill and dump' toy You could use a large plastic sweet jar (these are easily obtainable from shops that sell loose sweets) or some other type of plastic container. Any number of different items are suitable for filling and dumping: stickle bricks, coloured cotton reels, pegs, sponges cut into hand-sized pieces, old plastic hair curlers or plastic lids from various bottles and jars (make sure they are not small enough to be swallowed). Older babies will enjoy putting the items in the jar, then dumping them out and doing it all over again. As babies play, you can also tell them the Bible verses for today, or part of the story. (You may remember that this activity was suggested in *Bible Stuff: God Gives us Families/Here comes Christmas*. But the children will probably not! Perhaps you could change the items you fill your toy with, for variety.)

week 2

Toddlers

Paint with shaving foam This activity was recommended last week for 2s and 3s. As children enjoy 'finger-painting', talk with them about fun times at church. Tell them about Samuel helping Eli at church.

Make shape puzzles with wallpaper Try to obtain an old book of wallpaper samples. Choose three or four quite different patterns and cut out a 30 cm square from each one. Glue the wallpaper squares onto thin card. Cut two or three simple shapes (square, triangle, circle) from each square of wallpaper. Mix up the pieces and see if the children can match the shapes and patterns. As the children work on the puzzles, tell them the Bible verses for today.

Play with buckets, spades and stones You will need enough small stones or pebbles to fill a washing-up bowl. Make sure that they are smooth and clean. Put a couple of small buckets and spades with them and let the children enjoy filling the buckets with pebbles and then dumping them out. Supervise closely to prevent the children from throwing stones or putting them in their mouths. As you talk to the children, try to include today's Bible story or some of the Bible verses.

2s - 3s

Clean the room Provide several dusting cloths and a spray bottle with water in it. Let children clean some of the surfaces in the room. Supervise this activity carefully, particularly the use of the water spray. In addition, let the children use a child-sized broom and dustpan. Place all the items in the home corner. As children clean, talk to them about things Samuel did to help Eli. Samuel may well have swept floors or polished candlesticks.

Play with a tunnel Arrange to borrow a play tunnel, or make your own by taping together three or four sturdy cardboard boxes. Children usually enjoy crawling through things. This activity may become noisy, so you may want to limit the amount of time it is available. It has no clear link with today's theme, but it is part of making church a happy experience.

Print with cotton reels You will need two or three empty cotton reels, paper and paint in a shallow dish. Provide painting aprons and warm water for washing hands. Put a folded piece of kitchen roll in the dish before you pour the paint in - this should make an effective printing pad. Some children will make neat prints with the reels, others will use them like brushes and smear them across the paper. There is not a right or a wrong way to do it. The children are making their own unique pictures. As children paint, be sensitive for opportunities to share Bible verses, part of the Bible story, or conversation related to today's teaching aim.

Make 'no-bake' oat cookies Inform parents in advance of this activity in case any of the children have allergies. Provide aprons and make sure the children wash their hands immediately before starting this activity. Bring a bowl and a wooden spoon for mixing. You may want to measure out the ingredients at home, and bring them in separate containers. Here is the recipe:

>3/4 cup* sugar
>75 g soft margarine
>2 cups* uncooked oats
>3 tablespoons cocoa
>1 tablespoon water
>1/2 teaspoon vanilla essence
>icing sugar
>
>* You can use a small to medium mug as a cup measure.

BIBLE STUFF   God Loves Children/Jesus is our Friend

Week 2

Stir together all the ingredients except the icing sugar. Roll the dough into small balls with your hands, then roll each ball in the icing sugar. (This recipe makes 15-20 cookies.)

Let the children take turns pouring in the various ingredients and stirring. When the dough is mixed, give each child a small spoonful to roll into a ball, then to roll in the icing sugar. Let them eat it straightaway.

This activity will require a lot of adult assistance, so you may want to do it as a group activity near the end of the session. Have the children tidy things away earlier than usual, then gather round to do this together.

This should be lots of fun (and very tasty!), and provide opportunity for good conversation about children helping and being part of things. Use Miriam and Samuel as illustrations as you talk with children.

3s - 5s

Let the children paint or print with cotton reels today, as well as cleaning the room with dusters and a spray bottle.

Place stones with the bricks Find six or seven stones of various shapes to put with bricks today. They should be at least as big as a lemon. Children are fascinated by the various colours and shapes of stones. Put them with the bricks and see how the children use them. Some will want to use them in what they are building, others will just enjoy looking at them.

Use lacing cards Make three or four cards for lacing. Punch holes around the edge of a rectangular piece of stiff card. Alternatively punch holes around the edge of pieces of card cut into the shape of a star, flower or basket. Provide shoelaces for the children to 'sew' with, or use lengths of thick wool with the ends wrapped with tape. As children 'sew' the cards, talk with them about Samuel and Eli, and also Miriam. Children learn as they hear things over and over again.

Sort leaves Bring several leaves from each of half a dozen different trees or bushes. Place the leaves together and let the children sort them by shape. Some children will find this easier than others. If they don't want to sort, they can simply enjoy looking at the leaves.

Group Time

2s - 3s

Let the children tell you about what they have done today. If you have made the cookies just before group time, they may be a little excited and need to sing a few movement songs to settle them down. After you have told the story, ask the children if any of them would like to pray. If not, say a prayer yourself. Thank God that we can love him and that we can do things to help others. As you wait for parents to come you could get the tunnel out again and let the children take turns crawling through it.

3s - 5s

Use the leaves to call the children to group time. Give out differently shaped leaves to each of the children. Keep a set of matching leaves for yourself. Hold these up one at a time and invite the child who has the matching leaf to come and sit in the circle.

Finish your group time today with a 'What's missing?' game. Collect about ten small objects which you can lay out on the floor in front of you - a toothbrush, a crayon, a brick, a peg, a spoon, etc. Ask the children to name each object, then to close their eyes. Take away one object and hide it. Let the children open their eyes and ask them to raise their hand if they know what is missing. If they find one missing object is too easy, take away two objects. You can play this game as parents arrive.

BIBLE STUFF — God Loves Children/Jesus is our Friend

GOD LOVES CHILDREN — WEEK 2

Take Home!

SAMUEL LOVED GOD
(1 SAMUEL 3)

Aim
To help the children understand that children can love God and can do things to help at church.

Bible verses
Samuel helped Eli at church. (1 Samuel 3:1)
Samuel wanted to do the things that made God happy. (1 Samuel 2:26)
The people knew that Samuel loved God and that he helped at church. (1 Samuel 3:19,20)

The story
Samuel was a boy who loved God. He helped Eli the teacher at church. Samuel learned about God from Eli.

One night Samuel heard someone call his name. He ran to Eli and said, 'Here I am. What do you need?' But Eli had not called Samuel. Eli said, 'I did not call you. Go back and lie down.'

Samuel went back to lie down. But he heard his name again. He went back to Eli, but it was not Eli who had called his name. Again, Samuel heard his name. This time when he went to Eli, the teacher knew that it was God talking to Samuel. Eli said, 'Go back and lie down. When you hear your name called again, say, "I am listening, God. What do you want to say to me?"'

Samuel did what Eli said. He loved God and wanted to do the things God wanted. As Samuel grew up, lots of people were his friends. They knew that he loved God and wanted to please God. Samuel stayed at the church to help Eli. As he grew up, he learned more about God.

Activity suggestions
Take a 'tour' round your church
Take your child for a look round your church during the week. (If you do not have your own building, you could take your child to see how your venue is used during the week.) Let them look at parts of the building they don't normally see. Talk about what different people do to help at church. If practical, offer to help in some small aspect of the cleaning or gardening, and let your child help you. If you have a young baby, you can put them where they can see you as you clean or garden.

Go stone collecting
Take your child for a walk and let them collect stones. Take a bag or basket to carry them in. When you get home, wash the stones together. Your child may enjoy playing with the stones with building bricks or cars. You may want to place a limit on the stones being in the house by saying 'You can play with these for two days, then we will take them back outside.'

BIBLE STUFF

God Loves Children   Week 3

NAAMAN'S SLAVE GIRL (2 KINGS 5:1-14)

Aim To help the children understand that children can help grown-ups; that children can know about God.

Preparation

The ministry of the prophet Elisha is the context of this story. Elisha, Naaman and Gehazi are its key players. We are not told the name of Naaman's slave girl, but once again we see a child (or young person) playing a key role in God's plan.

Naaman was a general in the Syrian army. Although he had won many honours, his success was clouded by leprosy. In the Old Testament the word 'leprosy' covers a range of skin diseases, all of which involved being a social outcast. Lepers were considered ceremonially unclean.

In one of the many skirmishes between Syria and Israel, a young Israelite girl had been captured. She served as a slave to Naaman's wife. She saw the sadness and discomfort Naaman suffered because of his leprosy. So she suggested to her mistress that Naaman go and visit 'the prophet' in Samaria.

Naaman's wife reported this conversation to her husband. For some reason, he decided to take the girl's advice. Perhaps he was willing to try anything. The rest of the story makes interesting reading, but we are particularly interested in the role of the slave girl. There must have been many similar incidences in the ministry of Elisha. For some reason, this one is deemed important enough to be recorded.

For our purposes, it provides us with another glimpse of the part children and young people had to play in the history of God's people. The writer could have told us that Naaman heard about Elisha and went to see him. But instead, he points out the link - an Israelite slave girl in a foreign land is true to her God, and is not ashamed to share what she knows. If it had not been for the girl, Naaman would not have been cured of his leprosy.

As a result of his healing, Naaman was ready to worship Yahweh as the only true God. This was quite an insight from a man who lived in a society of many gods. So the slave girl was instrumental not only in Naaman's healing, but also in his journey of faith.

Two things should encourage us here. Firstly, being anonymous doesn't minimize the role you can play in what God is doing. Secondly, children have a significant role to play in God's scheme of things. Taking these two things to their logical conclusion means that passing on the faith to under fives is an important ministry.

'Lord, help me to make the most of every opportunity today. Help me to demonstrate your love, to communicate biblical truths, and to help each of the children in their development. Help me to teach in both words and actions. In Jesus' name, Amen.'

Story Time

Bible verses
Naaman's slave girl knew that God could make Naaman well. (2 Kings 5:3)
Help one another. (Galatians 5:13)

Week 3

Birth - 2s

Naaman was an important man. He was a general in the army. But Naaman was sick.

There was a slave girl in Naaman's house. She worked for Naaman's wife. The slave girl loved God. She told Naaman's wife about a man who loved God who could help Naaman get well.

Naaman went to see the man. The man told Naaman what to do. Naaman wasn't sick any longer.

Naaman was very happy. He said to the man, 'I know that the God you love is the real God. I want to love him, too.'

Naaman's slave girl loved God. She helped Naaman to get well and to know about God, too.

3s - 5s

Naaman was an important man. He was a general in the army. But Naaman was sick. He had a disease in his skin called leprosy. It made Naaman sad.

Naaman's army had captured some people in a battle. One of the girls who was captured lived in Naaman's house. She was a slave who worked for Naaman's wife.

The slave girl loved God. She told Naaman's wife about a man who loved God who could help Naaman get well.

Naaman went to see the man. He told Naaman to dip in the river seven times and he would be well. Naaman thought that was a silly thing to do. But he decided to do it anyway.

When he did it, Naaman was made well. He was very happy. He said to the man, 'Now I know that the God you love is the real God. I want to love him, too.'

Naaman's slave girl loved God. She helped Naaman to get well and to know about God, too.

Teaching Activities

As we continue this unit, let's ask God to help us see each child we teach through the eyes of the Holy Spirit. We want to be sensitive to the needs of every child. Some of those needs are obvious, others are not. God wants to use us as instruments of his love and peace into even the youngest lives today.

Babies

Make a 'picture tube' Look in magazines for pictures of children of a variety of ages. Cut them out and glue them onto a cardboard tube which you have covered with plain paper. You may be able to re-cycle a cylinder which was used as packaging for crisps or biscuits. Babies can hold the tube or roll it around and look at the pictures. As they do so, tell them about Naaman's slave girl, and also about Samuel and Miriam.

Play in a tunnel This activity was suggested for 2s - 3s last week. You may be able to use the same tunnel or make one as suggested there. Obviously, this activity is for older babies who are able to crawl, but even younger babies may enjoy watching.

Water play Use a baby bath or a washing-up bowl with a few centimetres of warm water in it. Cover the immediate floor area with newspaper. You can sit next to a baby on the floor, or you may find it easier to hold the baby on your lap while he or she splashes fingers in the water. You might want to put one or two items that float in the water for babies to grab at. This activity need not be limited to the older babies. Even young babies can be held while they enjoy splashing fingers in water. Water activities require very close supervision. As they enjoy the water, sing to babies or tell them verses from the Bible. Thank God for water.

Week 3

Toddlers

Wash the dishes Put a few centimetres of warm soapy water in a washing-up bowl and provide several tea towels (for wiping dishes and mopping up spills!). Let the children wash the dishes that you use in the home corner. You will need to cover their clothes with plastic aprons, and the floor with a plastic sheet or several layers of newspaper. Let the children take turns washing and wiping. This is an important part of learning to share. Talk to the children about helping. Tell them about how Naaman's slave girl helped.

Colour with crayons Provide several chunky crayons and paper for children to colour on. You might want to cut the paper in a different shape today, perhaps a triangle. Some children may make one or two marks on a piece of paper, then ask for another one. It may be helpful to set limits: a child may make one picture, and then do something else. This helps the children learn about sharing and about not wasting resources.

It's good for children to learn that there are limits on their activities. Of course they will fight those limits and push them as hard as they can. But knowing that there is a limit which will be upheld is actually a source of security for children. They are often unable to control or limit themselves, so knowing that a grown-up is there to do it for them gives them freedom.

Make instant whip You will need a mixing bowl, large spoon, one or two packets of instant whip (vanilla or strawberry flavour), a whisk, and cups and spoons for each child. One packet should make enough for eight children. They should wash their hands immediately before starting this activity. Let the children help pour in the milk and the instant whip powder. Let each child have a turn with the whisk, if they want. As you work together to make the instant whip you can share Bible verses, or talk about children helping. You could even sing - it helps the children who are waiting their turn to be more patient. When the whip is ready, spoon some into a cup for each child. A few spoonfuls is enough - this isn't their lunch! Make sure you put a sign on the door notifying parents of what you are doing so that they can alert you to any food allergies.

2s - 3s

Play with buckets, spades and small stones This activity was suggested for toddlers last week.

Make a collage of paper shapes Cut pieces of coloured paper into simple shapes such as squares, circles and triangles. Cut some irregular shapes as well. Let the children glue shapes onto a piece of white paper in any way they want. Some will make recognizable pictures, others will just enjoy the experience of gluing. The important thing is to let each child work as independently as possible. As the children work you can talk or sing about the theme for today.

String beads Provide a set of wooden beads for stringing. You can make a set from empty cotton reels, with shoelaces for stringing. Some children will be adept at this, but others will find it quite a difficult task. Be ready to assist and encourage those who need help.

Play with a doctor's kit Make up a medical kit for children to play with. You can put the items in a plastic container with a lid. Include one or two wrap bandages, some cotton wool, a few empty plastic medicine bottles without lids and a triangle bandage to make a sling if you have one. (Do not put sweets into a bottle for 'pretend' tablets.) Place the kit in the home corner. Children may want to play doctor with the doll, or even a teacher. As the children play, talk about Naaman being ill and his slave girl telling him where to go to get better. You may also remind the children never to take medicine from bottles by themselves, but only when a grown-up gives it to them.

Week 3

3s - 5s

Make a paper shape collage with 3s - 5s today. Provide plenty of shapes. You can always keep the leftovers for another time.

Wallpaper puzzles You will find instructions for making wallpaper puzzles in last week's Toddler section. Cut four or five different shapes in each puzzle for this older age group. As children work the puzzles, tell them about Naaman's slave girl. Use today's Bible verses in conversation.

Provide musical instruments If you do not already have a set of children's instruments, you may be able to borrow one from a local play group. Put the instruments on the floor and let the children come and play them. Sing songs for them to 'accompany'. Make up one or two songs about the stories in this unit. The children probably won't sing as they play - doing both things at once is quite a feat of co-ordination for such young children!

Go outside If it is fine take the children outside. Take them all together for fifteen minutes during the session or you may find it easier to have two adults taking two or three children at a time throughout the session. (The recommended supervision ratio for outdoor activities is one adult to two children.) Take a ball for the children to play with, or let them 'water paint'. Fill paint pots with water. Give out chunky brushes and let the children 'paint' on the path or on a wall. (Avoid painting on wooden surfaces which may splinter.) They will be interested to see how quickly the water disappears if it is a warm day. As you enjoy being outside, thank God for the world he has made. It is good for the children to hear our spontaneous prayers of thanks.

Make oat cookies You will find the recipe and instructions for this activity in last week's 2s - 3s section.

Group Time

2s - 3s

Play a game to call children to the circle today. Give each child one of the paper shapes left over from the collage activity. Call out a colour and let the children holding paper of the same colour come to the circle. Continue until all the children are seated. Collect the paper shapes. As you tell the Bible story today you may be able to review the stories from the last two weeks. It will, of course, depend on the attentiveness of the children. They learn by repetition, so it never hurts to go over stories again.

As you wait for parents, continue the 'bucket and spade' theme of the session as you roll or throw a beach ball with the children.

3s - 5s

You can use the same ideas at group time as listed for 2s - 3s today. At the end you can bring out the musical instruments again rather than a beach ball.

GOD LOVES CHILDREN WEEK 3

Take Home!

NAAMAN'S SLAVE GIRL (2 KINGS 5:1-14)

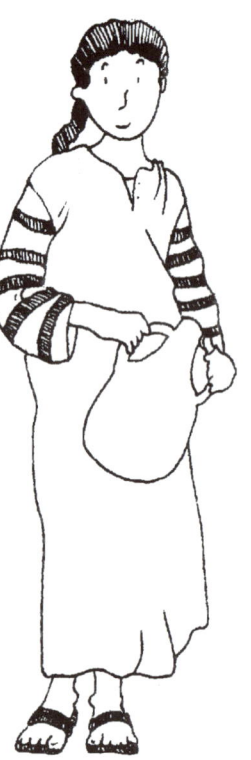

Aim
To help the children understand that children can help grown-ups; that children can know about God.

Bible verses
Naaman's slave girl knew that God could make Naaman well. (2 Kings 5:3)
Help one another. (Galatians 5:13)

The story
Naaman was an important man. He was a general in the army. But Naaman was sick. He had a disease in his skin called leprosy. It made Naaman sad.

Naaman's army had captured some people in a battle. One of the girls who was captured lived in Naaman's house. She was a slave who worked for Naaman's wife.

The slave girl loved God. She told Naaman's wife about a man who loved God who could help Naaman get well.

Naaman went to see the man. He told Naaman to dip in the river seven times and he would be well. Naaman thought that was a silly thing to do. But he decided to do it anyway.

When he did it, Naaman was made well. He was very happy. He said to the man, 'Now I know that the God you love is the real God. I want to love him, too.'

Naaman's slave girl loved God. She helped Naaman to get well and to know about God, too.

Activity suggestions
Make a picture tube or box for your baby
Look in magazines for pictures of children of a variety of ages. Cut them out and glue them onto a cardboard tube or box which you have covered with plain paper.

As your baby holds the tube or rolls it around they can look at the pictures. Talk to them about Naaman's slave girl, and also about Samuel and Miriam.

Make 'no-bake' oat cookies with your child
Your child may have been involved in making these during the session this week or last week. Here is the recipe for you to use at home. Use a medium-sized cup to measure sugar and oats.

3/4 cup sugar
75 g soft margarine
2 cups uncooked oats
3 tablespoons cocoa
1 tablespoon water
1/2 teaspoon vanilla essence
icing sugar

Stir together all the ingredients except the icing sugar. Roll the dough into small balls with your hands, then roll each ball in the icing sugar. (This recipe makes 15-20 cookies.)

BIBLE STUFF

God Loves Children   week 4

JESUS AND THE CHILDREN
(MATTHEW 19:13-15; MARK 10:13-16)

Aim To help the children understand that Jesus loves and values children.

 ## Preparation

This story shows us what Jesus thinks about children, and helps us to understand their place in God's kingdom.

It is easy to imagine the scene. Wherever Jesus went, people were healed and made whole simply by his touch. His hands were an instrument of blessing. No wonder the mothers brought their children to Jesus. Of course they wanted his hands to touch them.

In the first century, children were not valued much until they were old enough to be of some use. People wanted to have children not so they could enjoy interacting with them and watching them grow, but so that they would have help in the family business and someone to look after them in their old age.

If people wanting to see Jesus were ranked in order of importance, the children would have been near the end of the queue. So it is understandable that the disciples turned them away. The disciples were Jesus' 'minders'. It was their job to protect Jesus from unnecessary disturbance. They weren't child-haters, they were simply trying to look after the Master, who was always surrounded by throngs of people.

When Jesus intervened, and asked the children to come to him, he was teaching something important about kingdom values - a person's worth is not based on what he can do, but on the fact that he (or she) is created by God. Jesus gave the children a position of great prominence by saying that adults needed to become like children in order to receive the kingdom of God.

Jesus did not mean that only children could receive the kingdom of God. He seemed to be saying that as adults we must become receptive and ready to trust, just like children.

In this story, Jesus was doing something he often did - giving dignity and value to those for whom society had little time. He did it by touching lepers, by eating with the 'riff-raff', by not stoning the woman caught in adultery. Here Jesus did it by embracing the children, giving them his blessing and saying that they had something to teach adults about openness to God.

In our society we think we are enlightened. When it comes to children, we 'talk a good game'. But many children in our communities are not truly valued. They are 'fobbed off' with expensive toys and games. They are given many privileges and opportunities. On the surface they have everything. But what they really long for is what Jesus gave the children that day - his time, his touch, his attention.

True dignity and worth do not come from material things. Children know they are valued when we spend time with them, look them in the eye and are happy just to 'be' with them. This is a gift we can give the children we teach week by week.

> 'Lord, please help me today to show your love in the same way you did - by taking time for each child, communicating through words and actions. Amen.'

BIBLE STUFF

Week 4

Story Time

Bible verses
Jesus said, 'Let the children come to me.' (Matthew 19:14)
Jesus loved the children. (Mark 10:16)

Birth - 2s
One day some mothers brought their children to see Jesus. There were lots of people who wanted to see Jesus.

Jesus' helpers thought that he would be too busy to talk to the children. So they told the mothers to take the children away. But Jesus saw them and said, 'Please don't send them away. Please bring the children to me.'

The children came to Jesus. He hugged them and put his hands on their heads. He told them that God loved them.

Jesus loved the children. He told the grown-ups that children are important to God.

The children must have been glad they got to see Jesus that day.

3s - 5s
One day some mothers brought their children to see Jesus. There were always lots of people who wanted to see Jesus. Jesus' helpers thought that he would be too busy to see the children. They said to the mothers, 'Jesus doesn't have time for your children. Please take them away.'

But Jesus heard what they said. He was sad that they thought he was too busy. Jesus said, 'Please don't send the children away. Please bring them to me.'

The children came to Jesus. He hugged them and put his hands on their heads. He told them that God loved them.

Jesus looked at the grown-ups. He said, 'Children are important. They know how to love God. You should be like them and love God, too.'

Jesus loved the children. The children must have been glad they were able to see Jesus that day

Teaching Activities

Let's ask God to help us truly value the children we teach, and to communicate that to them effectively. Let's give them our time, make eye contact with them and let them know they are important to us and to God.

Babies
Make a picture book of babies and children Cut out pictures of young children and babies from old magazines or catalogues. Mount them on cards and punch holes along the side of each card so you can tie the pages together to make a book. Show the pictures to a baby as you hold him or her on your lap; talk to the baby about Jesus and the children. You may want to use the book you made in Week 1 as well.

BIBLE STUFF   God Loves Children/Jesus is our Friend **20**

Week 4

Play with large building bricks Let babies play today with a set of large plastic stacking bricks. Alternatively make your own set from shoe boxes, cereal boxes or other cardboard containers of an appropriate size. Stuff them with newspaper so they won't crush easily, then cover them with coloured paper. As babies play with the stacking toys, sing songs about Jesus. If you can make up simple songs, do so. Otherwise you can sing the chorus 'Yes, Jesus loves me, the Bible tells me so'.

Colour with crayons For older babies provide a few chunky crayons in bright colours and some paper. You may need to guide their hands at first until they realize how to make marks on the paper. Of course, they will only make scribbles, but that is the first stage of artistic expression!

Toddlers

Use a picture book of babies and children for toddlers today. Rather than making it beforehand, bring all the materials and let the children help you put it together by gluing the pictures on the card. Let the children play in a tunnel as suggested for other age groups during the last two weeks.

Sand play with stones and shells Provide dry sand in a large plastic container such as a washing-up bowl or a baby bath. Put a plastic sheet or newspaper on the floor under the sand area. Add some large shells and stones to the sand. You may want to bury them under the sand so the children can feel around and find them. Always supervise sand play very carefully. As the children play, tell them about the children going to see Jesus.

2s - 3s

Look at books about Jesus Put out four or five books about Jesus today. You may already have some in your supplies. If you are going to buy new ones, choose books with strong covers, simple and realistic pictures, and not too many words. Why not try to create a special book corner? If possible, arrange for an adult to stay in this area to allow for quiet reading to children. You could invite someone from your church to come in to read to children. As children enjoy the books, they will also enjoy the time that the reader is able to spend with them. Tell them about Jesus having time for children.

Water play with animals Cover the water play area with newspaper to absorb spills. Put a few centimetres of water in a washing-up bowl or baby bath. Put four or five toy animals in the water - sea creatures, if possible.

Easel paint Provide two or three colours of paint today. Or try using white paint on coloured paper. Take time to talk with children as they paint. Tell them about Jesus and the children, or sing to them about Jesus. Some children will relish the attention. But do be sensitive - there are some children who prefer to be quiet when they are painting.

Sort flowers by colour Bring an assortment of flowers and let the children sort them by colour. If you don't have easy access to real flowers, cut flower shapes from different colours of paper. Provide four or five in each colour for the children to sort, in as many as six different colours.

Go outside Take a beach ball outside to play with, or let the children water paint on the path or other suitable surfaces, as recommended for 3s - 5s last week. The recommended supervision ratio for outdoor activities is one adult to two children.

3s - 5s

Provide books about Jesus for 3s - 5s today. You may also want to invite a visitor to come and sit with the children in the book area today. If you want to include sand play with stones and shells you will find instructions in this week's Toddlers section.

Week 4

Wash dishes Let the children wash the dishes from the home corner. Provide a bowl of warm soapy water and several tea towels. The child who is washing may need to wear a plastic apron, and you will want to cover the floor with newspaper to absorb spills. Let the children take turns washing and wiping. As children work together tell them about Jesus and the children.

String beads If you do not have a set of beads for stringing, you may be able to borrow some, or make up a set as suggested for 2s and 3s last week. Some children can do this easily, but others will need your help and patience as this requires good co-ordination of small muscles.

Paint with shapes From stiff cardboard cut out two triangles, two squares and two circles (side and diameter approximately 5 cm). Vary the sizes slightly if you wish. Put a small cardboard tag on the back of each one so that it can be held by a clothes peg.

Provide two colours of paint in shallow dishes. Put some folded kitchen towel in each dish to absorb the paint and act as a printing pad. Let the children press a cardboard shape into the paint, then press it on their paper.

Group Time

A useful resource for general songs is the tape 'God's Wonderful World' by Julia Plant and Lucy East (Peony Records, Kingsway), containing sixteen action songs on classical instruments for ages 0-8.

2s - 3s

Use the flowers for an opening activity. Give them out to the children and let them see who has matching colours. When you are ready to sing or tell the story, collect the flowers so that the children will not be distracted by them.

Today's story is one that children respond to well. As you finish telling it you could say, 'Jesus loved the children; Jesus loves you.' Go around the circle and say this to each child by name. Some children will meet your gaze, others will not, but all children like to hear their name. And how important for each child to know that Jesus loves him or her as an individual!

As you wait for parents you can read the books about Jesus to the children.

3s - 5s

Use a movement song to prepare the children for listening to the Bible story. Use the tune of 'Here we go round the mulberry bush' and sing: 'It's fun to walk around the room, around the room, around the room. It's fun to walk around the room with our friends.' Lead the children around the room as you sing. Substitute 'march', 'hop', 'skip' and other actions for 'walk'. Sing the song several times.

As suggested for 2s - 3s, make a point of saying to each child, 'Jesus loves you.' At the end, read the books about Jesus to the children as you wait for parents to arrive.

BIBLE STUFF   God Loves Children/Jesus is our Friend   22

GOD LOVES CHILDREN — WEEK 4

Take Home!

JESUS AND THE CHILDREN
(MATTHEW 19:13-15; MARK 10:13-16)

Aim
To help the children understand that Jesus loves and values children.

Bible verses
Jesus said, 'Let the children come to me.'
(Matthew 19:14)
Jesus loved the children. (Mark 10:16)

The story
One day some mothers brought their children to see Jesus. There were always lots of people who wanted to see Jesus. Jesus' helpers thought that he would be too busy to see the children. They said to the mothers, 'Jesus doesn't have time for your children. Please take them away.'

But Jesus heard what they said. He was sad that they thought he was too busy. Jesus said, 'Please don't send the children away. Please bring them to me.'

The children came to Jesus. He hugged them and put his hands on their heads. He told them that God loved them.

Jesus looked at the grown-ups. He said, 'Children are important. They know how to love God. You should be like them and love God, too.'

Jesus loved the children. The children must have been glad they were able to see Jesus that day.

Activity suggestions
Look at or read books about Jesus
Whatever the age of your child, you can enjoy books together. Even if your baby is very young, he or she will look at pictures. Hearing you talk about Jesus is an important part of a baby's growing understanding of the Christian faith.

If you do not have any books about Jesus, you may be able to borrow some from your church, or from a family in your church. Have a special reading time with your child. Include telling the story of Jesus and the children. You may want to open your own Bible to Matthew 19 as you tell your child about it.

Sort flowers by colour
Cut out simple flower shapes from different coloured pieces of paper. If you don't have coloured paper, use plain paper, then colour the shapes with crayons or pencils. Toddlers will only need three or four colours. Older under fives may be able to manage six or eight colours. Make several shapes of each colour, then help your child sort them. Of course, if your garden is in full bloom, you may be able to do this with real flowers! As you spend time together, you can talk about Jesus and the children.

Jesus is our Friend

week 1

JESUS FEEDS THE PEOPLE (MARK 6:30-44, JOHN 6:1-14)

Aim To help the children understand that Jesus was special; that Jesus cared about people's practical needs - he fed them when they were hungry.

Preparation

The feeding of the five thousand must have made a big impression on Jesus' disciples because it is the only miracle which is recorded in all four of the Gospels. It is a good story to use with young children because they can easily understand it. They know about being hungry and they know about eating. This story clearly demonstrates Jesus' interest in the practical as well as the spiritual side of life. It also demonstrates that Jesus could do things that no one else could do.

This story has many aspects, but let's ask God to challenge us on two things. Firstly, there is the example of Andrew. Yet again, he was bringing someone to Jesus (see John 1:41,42). When he found the lad with his small lunch he didn't say, 'Well, this will never be enough so I won't bother.' His actions said, 'This isn't much, but maybe Jesus can do something with it.'

When Andrew brought the boy to Jesus he had no idea what Jesus was going to do. When you and I bring people to Jesus, we don't know what he will do. As we teach children week by week, as we bring up our own children in the faith, and as we bring others to Jesus through the ministry of our lives, who knows what he will do with them? It is a challenge and an encouragement to be faithful in bringing people to Jesus, so that he can do miraculous things in them and even through them.

The second challenge comes from the lad himself. If he hadn't given what he had to Jesus, the people would not have been fed. He was unselfish, willing to share. He had faith - he didn't let the smallness of what he had prevent him from offering it to Jesus.

We, too, must give whatever we have and whatever we are to Jesus. It may not seem like much to us. But if five loaves and two fishes can feed thousands of people, then the gifts and abilities we have can surely be multiplied by Jesus as well.

May God encourage us to keep on faithfully bringing people to Jesus. And may we unreservedly and joyfully give what we have - and what we are - to him, so that he can turn it into so much more than we ever could.

'Lord Jesus, show me again this week what it means for you to be the Bread of Life to me. Help me to know in new ways what it means for you to satisfy my heart. Fill me to overflowing so that I can teach from fulness of Spirit this week. I pray this so that your name may be glorified, Amen.'

Story Time

Bible verses
Jesus went about doing good. (Acts 10:38)
Jesus loved the people who came to him. (Mark 6:34)
Jesus fed the people fish and bread. (John 6:11)

Week 1

Birth - 2s

Lots of people had come to see Jesus. He wanted to teach them about God. They listened to him talk. After a while, the people were getting hungry. Jesus asked his helpers if they could feed the people.

They said to him, 'There are too many people. We don't have any food. We don't have enough money to buy food for all these people.'

One boy had brought his lunch with him. He had some bread and some fish. He gave it to Jesus.

Jesus said 'thank you' to God, then he started passing out the bread and the fish. There was enough for everybody. There was even some left at the end.

Jesus had fed all the people. Now they were not hungry.

3s - 5s

Jesus and his helpers went across the lake in a boat. When they got to the other side, there were lots of people waiting for them.

When Jesus saw the people, he loved them. He knew they wanted to hear about God. So he started to teach them.

After a while, the people were getting hungry. Jesus asked his helpers if they could feed the people.

They said to him, 'There are too many people. We don't have any food. Even if we went to buy some, we don't have enough money to buy food for all these people.'

Andrew, one of Jesus' helpers, brought a boy to Jesus. The boy had brought some lunch. He had some bread rolls and some fish. But it was only enough for him.

The boy gave his food to Jesus. Jesus said 'thank you' to God, then he started passing out the bread and the fish. As they passed out the food, they found there was enough for everybody. All the people had bread and fish to eat. There was even some left over at the end.

Jesus loved the people. He had fed all the people. Now they were not hungry.

Teaching Activities

Jesus met the people's physical need - they were fully satisfied. When Jesus meets our spiritual needs, we are fully satisfied. As we teach this morning, let's pray that we will know a fulness of Spirit that comes from being fed by Jesus. Then we can naturally and gladly teach the children about Jesus being very special.

Babies

Sing songs about Jesus In this unit we can sing, sing, sing to the children about Jesus! Use the chorus of 'Jesus loves me'. If you know it, use the chorus, 'Oh how I love Jesus'. Make up your own songs, using words about Jesus loving us, us loving him and about Jesus being our friend. Make up a song about Jesus feeding the people - use very simple words like, 'Jesus fed the people, he gave them fish and bread.' You can make up a song about the story each week in this unit. Babies enjoy music, and they aren't bothered about the tunefulness of your voice!

BIBLE STUFF   God Loves Children/Jesus is our Friend

Week 1

Look at a book about food Look through magazines to find five or six pictures of food. Try to find simple and clear pictures of items such as fruit, vegetables, a loaf of bread and a bottle of milk. Many supermarkets have free leaflets which may be a good source of pictures. Cut them out and glue them onto pieces of card to make a board book for babies to look at. Older babies can handle the book. You can show the pictures to younger babies as they sit on your lap or lie in their buggies and prams. Tell them about Jesus feeding the people as they look at the pictures.

Make shakers that roll Collect a few empty canisters to make into shakers. Containers for drinking chocolate, cocoa, custard powder or even the taller ones that contain crisps would all be suitable. Choose from dried beans, pasta, lentils or rice to place inside to give each shaker a different sound. Cover the outside of the canisters with coloured paper, or patterned sticky-backed plastic. Glue or tape the lid on securely. Shake or roll the canisters for younger babies. Older ones will enjoy doing it themselves.

Play with saucepans Bring two or three saucepans, a colander and some wooden spoons for babies to play with. They can 'stir', stack the saucepans, or even drum the pans and colander with the wooden spoon. As they play, you can talk to them or sing to them about Jesus.

Toddlers

Try to use lots of songs with toddlers today, and through this whole unit. Make a book of food pictures, too. If the pictures are simple enough, you might want to print the name of the food on each page. Toddlers will also enjoy the home-made shakers.

Make a food collage Cut out pictures of food from magazines - enough for each child to glue three or four. Provide a piece of paper for each child. Let them choose one picture at a time and help them glue it on their paper. You may need to spread glue on the back of the picture, but try to let each child place it on the paper themselves. Don't worry if they glue one picture on top of another - we're not giving points for artistic impression! When a child has finished, try to find a space on their paper to print 'Jesus fed the people'. If you write it on their paper beforehand, they will probably glue a picture over the words.

2s - 3s

Plan to use lots of songs with 2s and 3s today and in this unit. Even this age group will enjoy the rolling shakers suggested for babies; let the children glue pictures of food onto the shakers. Make individual pictures of food, or all work together to make a mural. Write 'Jesus fed the people' across the top of the mural. Put it outside the classroom after the session so that parents can look at it.

Look at cookery books Bring in two or three illustrated cookery books. Sit with the children as they look at the pictures. Talk about the foods they like. Tell them about Jesus feeding the people.

Taste bread and fish Bring bread and tinned tuna fish for children to taste. They should wash their hands immediately before starting this activity. Use a sliced loaf, or bring an uncut loaf to slice or even tear into chunks. Tuna in brine is less messy than tuna in oil. Invite each child to take a piece of bread and to spoon a small amount of tuna onto it. As they eat, tell them today's story. As with all activities involving food, notify parents in advance in case of allergies.

3s - 5s

The suggestions for 2s and 3s will work with this group as well today - songs, a food collage or mural, looking at cookery books and tasting bread and fish.

BIBLE STUFF

Week 1

You may also want to try the following activity:

Food puzzles Make puzzles from pictures of food. If you know someone who is involved in the catering business, they may be able to get you some outdated brochures which will contain large, colourful pictures of food. Alternatively you could ask at a supermarket for posters of food. If you go to the bakery section and fresh fish bar, you might even get pictures of bread and fish. If all else fails, you can probably find a few fairly big pictures of food from supermarket magazines. Mount the pictures on some card, then cut them up into four- or five-piece puzzles. You could cover the pictures with clear sticky-backed plastic before you cut them. This will make them more durable so that you can keep them and use them another time, if you have the storage space.

Group Time

The following songs could be used as part of your group time: 'Share it round' (tune of Frère Jacques) and 'Fish and bread' from *Feeling Good, Songs of Wonder and Worship*, Peter Churchill, National Society/CHP; 'One boy had two fish' (tune of Happy Birthday), 38, *100 Action Songs for Preschoolers*; 'Crunch, crunch, crunch, they ate my lunch', Sam Horner, Daybreak Music (on New Wine tape *Skipper's Nippers / Wake up and dance,* ICC).

2s - 3s

Use songs and conversation to settle the children into group time. You may want to ask them if they tasted the bread and fish. You can then say, 'I want to tell you a story from the Bible about Jesus feeding the people.' After you have told the story, say a prayer thanking God that Jesus could do things no one else could do. Thank God that Jesus loved the people.

As you wait for parents to arrive you can look at the cookery books. If you have several children and more than one teacher, let each teacher have a book and a small group of children around them so that everyone can see the pictures easily.

3s - 5s

The group time suggestions for 2s and 3s are also suitable for 3s - 5s today. If you have an outgoing group of children, you may want to let them act out the story after you have told it. Give one child a small basket and let him (or her) be the little boy. Let another child be Andrew. Let another child be Jesus. After Andrew brings the boy to Jesus and he hands over his lunch, all three of them can pretend to pass out food to the other children. If they enjoy this, do it again until all the children who want to have had a turn to 'act'.

JESUS IS OUR FRIEND — WEEK 1

Take Home!

JESUS FEEDS THE PEOPLE
(MARK 6:30-44; JOHN 6:1-14)

Aim
To help the children understand that Jesus was special; that Jesus cared about people's practical needs - he fed them when they were hungry.

Bible verses
Jesus went about doing good. (Acts 10:38)
Jesus loved the people who came to him. (Mark 6:34)
Jesus fed the people fish and bread. (John 6:11)

The story
Jesus and his helpers went across the lake in a boat. When they got to the other side, there were lots of people waiting for them.

When Jesus saw the people, he loved them. He knew they wanted to hear about God. So he started to teach them.

After a while, the people were getting hungry. Jesus asked his helpers if they could feed the people.

They said to him, 'There are too many people. We don't have any food. Even if we went to buy some, we don't have enough money to buy food for all these people.'

Andrew, one of Jesus' helpers, brought a boy to Jesus. The boy had brought some lunch. He had some bread rolls and some fish. But it was only enough for him.

The boy gave his food to Jesus. Jesus said thank you to God, then he started passing out the bread and the fish. As they passed out the food, they found there was enough for everybody. All the people had bread and fish to eat. There was even some left over at the end.

Jesus loved the people. He had fed all the people. Now they were not hungry.

Activity suggestions
Look at cookery books or food magazines together
Take a few minutes to sit with your child and look at cookery books or magazines (you can usually pick up free magazines and leaflets at supermarkets). Talk about foods you enjoy. Tell your child about Jesus feeding the people. If you can, take a slow walk round the greengrocer's, or even the fishmonger's, and talk about the great variety of taste and colour in food.

Taste fish and bread together
Perhaps as one of your meals this week you could have fish and bread. You might be able to make it special by eating in the garden or park (or in your lounge with a mat on the floor if it's raining). Any kind of fish will be fine (even fishfingers!). If you have a basket you can put it in, all the better. Do what you can to help your child 'live' the story. If it is appropriate, your whole family might be able to join in. Let your child serve the fish and/or bread. Tell the story as you eat together.

BIBLE STUFF — God Loves Children/Jesus is our Friend

Jesus is our Friend

Week 2

JESUS HEALS A BLIND MAN
(MARK 10:46-52, LUKE 18:35-43)

Aim To help the children understand that Jesus could do things no one else could do; that Jesus made sick people well.

Preparation

Here is another incident from Jesus' ministry that teaches us truth simply and clearly. As well as teaching the children about Jesus' power and compassion, it provides us with an opportunity to thank God for the gift of sight.

We can learn from Bartimaeus: he knew exactly what he wanted from Jesus, and he grabbed his chance when it came. He knew that Jesus could heal him, so he shouted out into the crowd. Jesus heard his cry and sent for him, asking what it was he wanted. Jesus often asked people what they wanted him to do for them. It wasn't that he didn't already know. He wanted people to articulate what they were looking for. We come to Jesus and he asks us, 'What do you want me to do for you?' Sometimes we stumble around, groping for an answer. Bartimaeus could have asked for money, or for food, or for any number of things. But he asked for the best. If he had not asked for his sight, he might not have received it.

Bartimaeus was one of the lowest members of his society, an outcast. He could have felt that he had no business asking Jesus for anything. That is certainly what the crowd felt. But he understood that, for Jesus, his worthiness was not an issue. Jesus was interested in him, and in his faith. We, too, may feel unworthy, but we can come to Jesus and dare to ask for the best. No request is too difficult for him. He can do exceedingly, abundantly, above all that we ask or even imagine.

As well as knowing what he wanted, Bartimaeus seized his opportunity. How often do we have a chance to ask something of Jesus, but we put it off? Maybe the time doesn't seem convenient. Maybe we are waiting for other things to happen. Bartimaeus' opportunity was literally a 'last chance'. Within days of this miracle, Jesus' earthly ministry had come to an end.

We must know what we want Jesus to do, we must dare to ask it, and we must take the opportunity when it comes. Waiting could mean we never have another chance quite like it.

As always, we can learn from Jesus. The road was busy with pilgrims on their way to Jerusalem for the Passover. As usual, he was surrounded by his disciples and other followers. They would have been pressing close, eager to hear him teach and talk as they went along. But when he heard the cry for help, Jesus stopped talking and started doing. Jesus' actions always matched his words. May God help us to be those whose 'walk lives up to their talk'.

As we teach children, we must not only say the words of the faith, we must also be the faith to the children in our care. Our words about Jesus must be matched by his love and compassion flowing through us.

'Even though Bartimaeus was blind, Lord, he still saw your power. Please help me not to be blind to what you want to do in and through my life. As I teach today, I pray that I may be able to help children "see" more of Jesus. Amen.'

BIBLE STUFF

God Loves Children/Jesus is our Friend

Week 2

Story Time

Bible verses
Jesus went about doing good. (Acts 10:38)
Jesus made a blind man see. (Mark 10:52)
The blind man knew that Jesus could make him well. (Luke 18:43)

Birth - 2s
Jesus was walking along the road. Lots of people were with him. Bartimaeus was sitting by the road. Bartimaeus could not see. But he heard all the people coming. He heard that Jesus was with them.

Bartimaeus shouted, 'Jesus, please help me!'

The people told him to be quiet. But he shouted even louder, 'Jesus, help me, please!'

Jesus said, 'Bring that man to me.'

When Bartimaeus was brought to Jesus he said, 'Please, Jesus, I want to be able to see.'

Jesus said, 'I'm glad that you know I can make you well. You can go now. You will be able to see.'

Bartimaeus was very happy that Jesus had made him well. Now he could see. He went with Jesus along the road.

3s - 5s
Jesus was walking along the road. Lots of people were with him.

A blind man named Bartimaeus was sitting by the side of the road. Bartimaeus could not see. But he could hear.

He heard the footsteps of all the people. He asked someone, 'What is happening?'

'It's Jesus,' they said. 'Jesus is walking by.'

Bartimaeus shouted out, 'Jesus, please help me!'

The people said, 'Shhh! Be quiet.'

But Bartimaeus shouted even louder, 'Jesus, help me, please!'

Jesus stopped walking. 'Bring that man to me,' he said.

Some men led Bartimaeus to Jesus. Jesus looked at him. 'What do you want me to do?' he asked.

'Please, Jesus,' said Bartimaeus. 'I want to be able to see.'

Jesus said, 'I am glad that you know I can make you well. You can go now. You will be able to see.'

Bartimaeus looked around. He could see! He was very happy that Jesus had made him well. He went along the road with Jesus.

Teaching Activities

As we teach today, we want to continue our emphasis on Jesus. But let's also thank God for our eyes, and for the wonderful gift of sight.

Babies
Let's continue to use the songs about Jesus that we sang last week. Here are some other ideas.

BIBLE STUFF

week 2

Look in a mirror Bring a mirror for babies to look at their reflections. If possible use a child's safety mirror. Of course, a baby will not recognize the connection between herself and what she sees in the mirror. But you can still say, 'Thank you, God, for Sarah's eyes. She can see herself in the mirror.' For older babies, bring a larger safety mirror that is free-standing or can lean against a wall. Babies can sit in front of it and look at themselves. Supervise this activity carefully.

Play peep-o Bring a tea towel or lightweight cloth or scarf to put over your face or a baby's face. For babies who are shy or wary, you may want just to hold the towel up between you and the baby. Older babies will pull the cloth away themselves because they know this game. As you play this familiar game, you can thank God for eyes to see, and talk about Jesus healing Bartimaeus.

Look at Bible pictures If you have a Bible with good pictures, hold it so that the babies can look at them. The International Children's Bible is worth looking at if you are thinking about buying one. If not, you may want to cut out simple colourful pictures from a magazine and mount them on card for babies to look at. Talk about the pictures and thank God for eyes. Thank God for Jesus, who made a blind man see.

Play with brightly coloured balloons Blow up two or three brightly coloured balloons and bounce them around for the babies to watch. Older babies may play with the balloons themselves. If so, don't inflate them too fully - popping balloons could create mayhem in a room full of babies! As the babies watch the balloons, thank God for eyes. Tell part of the story of Bartimaeus.

Toddlers
As with babies, continue to use lots of songs about Jesus.

In addition:
Mix coloured water You will need two or three clear plastic cups or bottles and a larger jug or bottle filled with water. Bring some red, yellow and blue food colouring. Pour water in the bottles or cups. Add a few drops of food colouring. Let the children watch the water change colour. Then combine two colours to see what other colours you can make. You will need a container into which you can empty the coloured water when you want to start again. Be careful not to refer to the process as magic. It isn't magic - it is the wonderful creativity of God! During this activity, thank God for all the beautiful colours he has made, and for eyes to see them. You may be able to tell the children about blind Bartimaeus.

Look at nature pictures Try to find some poster-sized pictures of animals, flowers or other nature scenes. Mount them on heavy card and cover them with clear sticky-backed plastic. (A local wildlife park, field-study centre or veterinary practice may be able to provide surplus posters or pictures.) Sit with the children and talk with them about the pictures as they look at them and touch them. Thank God for eyes.

Paint with bright colours Use an easel or paint at a low table. Provide two bright colours, chunky paint brushes and large sheets of paper. Make sure you cover clothes with an apron. Put a bowl of warm soapy water nearby with a towel for washing hands after painting. (If you add a small squirt of washing-up liquid to the paint, it will wash off hands and clothes more easily.) Sing about painting, or doing fun things at church during this activity. 'I like to paint at church; I like to paint at church. It's fun to paint with brushes; I like to paint at church' are suitable words - just make up a simple tune to go with them.

2s - 3s
Mixing coloured water and painting with bright colours are two activities you can use with 2s - 3s today. They will also enjoy looking at nature pictures.

Play with a doctor's kit in the home corner Use an empty plastic box to make a medical kit for the home corner. Put in it a few wrap bandages (if they are fairly long you may want to cut them in half to make them more manageable), some empty plastic medicine bottles and cotton wool. You can make pretend plasters by cutting 7 cm strips of masking tape and sticking a small square of white paper in the middle of each strip. Most children won't use these on themselves, but will put them on a doll. If you know someone who is a doctor or nurse, you may be able to get a mask like those worn in operating theatres.

Week 2

Many children will not want bandages wrapped around their own arms or legs, but will enjoy bandaging a teacher or a doll. As the children play doctor, tell them about Jesus making sick people well and about him making Bartimaeus able to see. (This activity was suggested previously in this unit. You may find it repetitive, but children learn through repetition. The addition of home-made plasters makes it slightly different.)

3s - 5s

The children will enjoy songs, and may want to sing with you as you sing about Jesus. They will also enjoy painting with bright colours.

Other activities are:

Play optician If you know someone who is an optician you may be able to borrow a wall chart and a 'patch' for covering one eye while testing the other. If not, you can make your own. Since children this young don't always know their letters, they use a wall chart with decreasing sizes of only a few letters: X, O, A, S, T, M, V. The child being tested has a card with those letters on it. The tester points to a letter on the chart and the child has to find the matching one on the card. This will require careful supervision. The children will probably enjoy it even if they don't quite get the testing right! The children will enjoy trying on 'play' glasses (frames without lenses in them). This activity provides great opportunity for talking about eyes and sight. You should be able to tell the children about Bartimaeus during this activity.

Work floor puzzles If you do not have any floor puzzles you may be able to borrow one from someone in your church. Try to get one that has a reasonably realistic picture - an animal or nature scene, for example, rather than a fantasy or cartoon character. Tell the Bible story as the children work on the puzzle. Also, talk to them about the Bible, as you tell them 'We work together' and 'We help one another'.

Plant seeds Bring a plastic cup or an empty yoghurt pot for each child, some potting compost, a large spoon and some seeds. Choose a variety that will germinate quickly - beans, for example. Cover the work area with newspaper so that children can spoon their own soil into a container. Moisten the soil after planting. As children work, you may be able to share today's Bible verses, or tell part of the story. Make sure that the children wash their hands after this activity.

The children can take the seeds home at the end of the session. If there are any special care instructions, you may want to photocopy one for each child, or write a large poster to place outside the room.

Group Time

2s - 3s

Start conversation in group time by looking again at the nature pictures. Invite the children to talk about what they have been doing during today's session. After you have told the story, prayed and sung, bring out two or three brightly coloured balloons for the children to keep in the air.

3s - 5s

Ask the children to stand together away from the group-time area. Call them one at a time by describing what they are wearing. Once all the children are seated you can begin conversation. Try also to include prayer, singing and the Bible story. As you wait for parents to arrive, let the children keep balloons in the air as suggested for 2s and 3s. Use only a few balloons - they are not for taking home. As children enjoy playing, continue teaching by thanking God for eyes to see the colours of the balloons.

BIBLE STUFF   God Loves Children/Jesus is our Friend

JESUS IS OUR FRIEND — WEEK 2

Take Home!

JESUS HEALS A BLIND MAN
(MARK 10:46-52, LUKE 18:35-43)

Aim
To help the children understand that Jesus could do things no one else could do; that Jesus made sick people well.

Bible verses
Jesus went about doing good. (Acts 10:38)
Jesus made a blind man see. (Mark 10:52)
The blind man knew that Jesus could make him well. (Luke 18:43)

The story
Jesus was walking along the road. Lots of people were with him.

A blind man named Bartimaeus was sitting by the side of the road. Bartimaeus could not see. But he could hear.

He heard the footsteps of all the people. He asked someone, 'What is happening?'

'It's Jesus,' they said. 'Jesus is walking by.'

Bartimaeus shouted out, 'Jesus, please help me!'

The people said, 'Shhh! Be quiet.'

But Bartimaeus shouted even louder, 'Jesus, help me, please!'

Jesus stopped walking. 'Bring that man to me,' he said.

Some men led Bartimaeus to Jesus. Jesus looked at him. 'What do you want me to do?' he asked.

'Please, Jesus,' said Bartimaeus; 'I want to be able to see.'

Jesus said, 'I am glad that you know I can make you well. You can go now. You will be able to see.'

Bartimaeus looked around. He could see! He was very happy that Jesus had made him well. He went along the road with Jesus.

Activity suggestions
Go for a 'colour walk' Whenever you are out walking with your baby or child, choose a different colour to look for. (If walking is not part of your normal routine, make special opportunities for that this week.) Look for things that are blue or yellow or pink. You may be surprised what an older child will see. For babies and toddlers, you will need to show them things of different colours. As you talk about various colours, thank God for eyes. Tell your child about Jesus and Bartimaeus.

For older under fives:
Help your child understand what it would be like not to see This may take different forms. Perhaps your child will close or cover their eyes and let you lead them through the house or garden. If your child is not frightened, you could go to the darkest place in your house so that they can experience what it is like to see nothing. Perhaps you know someone who is blind or partially sighted, or someone who trains guide dogs. Your local library may even have some books in Braille. The point is not to sadden or worry your child, but to help them understand what it might have been like for Bartimaeus. As you tell the story, you can thank God together for being able to see.

Jesus is our Friend   Week 3

JESUS TEACHES THE PEOPLE (MATTHEW 6:25-34; LUKE 12:22-31)

Aim To help the children understand that Jesus was special; that he taught the people about God's love.

Preparation

These almost identical passages are well known to most people who have been Christians for any length of time. But for children, these words will be fresh and new. They will speak clearly to them of God's love and care. Children under the age of five are not generally acquainted with the adult occupation of worry. So when they hear that Jesus told the people not to worry, they will take it at face value.

'If God takes care of the birds and flowers, then he will take care of me.' For children, this is a simple statement of fact. What better heritage could we give them than to grow up with that kind of trust! So let's help them to have that strong foundation - the certainty of God's love and care for them.

But what about you and me? Do we need to be reminded, yet again, not to put too much emphasis on what we eat and drink, or how fashionable our clothes are? Do we need a reminder that worry is an utter waste of time? We probably do.

Jesus isn't saying that we shouldn't care at all. Neither is he saying that we shouldn't be wise and careful about working hard and making sensible provision for the future. What he is attacking are two common human failings - traps which it's particularly easy for end-of-century Westerners to fall into.

The first trap is being too concerned about external things. We are easy prey to the fashion industry as it changes the 'look' each season, simply to make more money. Most of us eat more than we need to. We spend a high proportion of our income on food and drink - and then spend even more trying to get slim and stay fit!

The second trap is that of worry. We worry about the past, even though there is nothing we can do to change it. We worry about the future, expending time and energy thinking anxiously about things that will probably never even happen. If things in our past are wrong, we need to be forgiven. After that, God doesn't bring them up again and neither should we. We need to make prudent plans for the future, but not to waste time worrying about what might, or might not, happen.

Everything we know of God tells us we can trust him. So why do we display a lack of faith by being anxious? Of course God understands our real concerns about very difficult situations we sometimes face. In those times, he wants to assure us more than ever of his love and care. But it saddens God when our lives are slowed down, sometimes paralyzed, by worry about less important things.

Take time this week to read the passages again. Let God's Word and his Spirit challenge you where you are missing the mark and comfort you with the certainty of his love and care.

'This week, Father, help me to take time to hear the birds as they sing and watch them as they fly. As I do that, please help me to be thrilled again with your love and care for me. Amen.'

Story Time

Bible verses
Jesus taught people about God. (Matthew 5:1-2)
Jesus said, 'God knows the things you need.' (Luke 12:30)
Jesus told the people to love God more than anything else. (Matthew 6:33)

BIBLE STUFF

Week 3

Birth - 2s

Jesus was teaching the people about God. He told them, 'Look at the birds in the sky. They don't worry about putting lots of food in a cupboard so they will have enough. But God takes care of them. You are more important to him than the birds.

'Look at the flowers. They don't go to a shop to buy clothes. But they are beautiful - with so many different colours!

'If God takes such good care of the birds and the flowers, he will take care of you. He loves you very much.

'Don't worry about what you eat and what you will wear. The most important thing is to love God.'

Jesus wanted the people to know how much God loved them.

3s - 5s

Lots of people were with Jesus. They were asking him questions about money. Jesus wanted to teach them about God's love.

He said, 'Look at the birds in the sky. They find food to eat each day. But they don't worry about putting some away in a cupboard for another day. God takes care of them. You are more important to him than the birds.

'Look at the flowers. They don't go to a shop to buy clothes. They don't worry about what they look like. But they are beautiful - with so many different colours!

'If God takes such good care of the birds and flowers, he will certainly take care of you. He loves you very much.

'Don't worry about what you will eat and what you will wear. God knows what you need. The most important thing is to love him.'

Jesus taught the people about God. He wanted them to know how much God loved them.

Teaching Activities

Babies

Look at flowers Bring a few brightly coloured flowers for babies to look at. Hold them so that a young baby can see them. You could say, for example, 'God made the beautiful flowers. God loves you, Robert. He will take care of you.' With older babies, put the flowers on some paper on the floor. Let them touch the flowers. They will undoubtedly be too rough, but resist the temptation to use plastic flowers. Handling real flowers will be a good experience of enjoying the natural world. Supervise carefully so that babies do not put the flowers in their mouths.

Put bright markers at Bible verses Choose four or five bright colours of paper to make Bible markers. Write today's verses on them, and one or two others from this unit. Place each one in the Bible at the appropriate reference. Show babies the brightly coloured markers, then open the Bible and say to one, 'The Bible says...' and then read the verse.

Look at nature pictures This activity was suggested for toddlers last week.

And don't forget to sing! A suitable song would be: 'Thank you, God' (to the tune of 'The wheels on the bus'), Nursery Praise, Mothers' Union.

Week 3

Toddlers
Use Bible markers with toddlers today.

In addition:

Finger-paint with baby lotion You will need a wipe-clean tray and a bottle of baby lotion. Put aprons over the children's clothing and roll up sleeves. Squirt a small amount of lotion onto the tray and guide a toddler to spread it around with his or her fingers. Some children will hesitate at using one finger, others will want to use both hands! Some may prefer not to take part - don't push them. Some children enjoy experiences like this; others don't. When they are finished, they can rub the lotion into their hands. Wipe away any excess with tissues. As the children 'finger-paint', tell them about Jesus teaching the people.

Play with a tunnel Arrange to borrow a play tunnel, or make your own by taping together three or four sturdy cardboard boxes. As a child comes out of the tunnel you could say, for example, 'God loves you, Hannah', or 'God takes care of the birds and flowers; he will take care of you.'

Play with brightly coloured balloons Blow up two or three balloons. Let the children bounce them in the air. As they play, tell them about God's care for the birds and flowers and about his love for them.

2s - 3s
Play with 'surprise' playdough Make up some fresh playdough but don't put any colouring into it. You will need enough for there to be a golf-ball-sized piece for each child. Press your thumb into each ball; put three or four drops of food colouring into the depression, then close the dough over it. Use a variety of colours. As the children play with the dough, it will gradually change to the colour of the drops within. Provide plastic bags with labels, or margarine tubs with lids, for parents to take their children's dough home. As children squeeze and roll their dough, tell them about Jesus teaching the people.

Paint with roller-balls Use empty roll-on deodorant bottles as paint containers. Pop the ball off the top and put paint into the bottle. Make it slightly thinner than you normally would. Pop the ball back on and roll it across some paper until the paint comes through.

If you have more than one bottle, use different colours. Let the children roll the bottle across their paper to make a picture. Empty the bottles after use to prevent the paint from drying out and clogging the roller. Sing songs about Jesus to the children as they paint.

Look at gardening catalogues You will need two or three gardening catalogues. As you look at the colour and variety of flowers with the children, it will be very natural to tell them about Jesus' teaching. Thank God for the beauty of the flowers. Thank him for his love for us.

Sort buttons Bring an assortment of variously coloured pegs or buttons for the children to sort. If you know someone who sews regularly, they may have a 'button box' you can sort through. Try to provide a variety of shapes and textures as well. As they play with the buttons, you will have opportunities for conversation. Tell each child how much God loves him or her. Make sure the children are carefully supervised at all times during this activity.

Week 3

3s - 5s
Bring seed catalogues for the children to look at, as well as making the surprise playdough balls.

Two other activities you may want to include are:
Paint with sponges Cut up a sponge into 5 cm cubes. Attach a spring-type clothes peg to each one. The children can hold the peg, then dip the sponge into one or two colours of paint in a shallow container. Some children will want to dab the sponge on their paper, others will use it like a paint brush. As they paint, talk or sing to the children about Jesus teaching the people.

Play with a medical kit This activity was suggested last week for 2s and 3s.

Group Time

2s - 3s
Call the children to group time by describing in turn what each one is wearing. Look together at the pictures in a gardening catalogue as you prepare to tell the story. Use songs about Jesus and action rhymes at the end of group time. As children wait for their parents, hand out the bags of playdough. Allow them to take their dough out and play with it as they sit and wait.

3s - 5s
You will need a seed or gardening catalogue. Cut out pictures of flowers in a variety of colours. Give them out before group time begins. You can then call the children to group time by saying, for example, 'Come to the circle if you have a picture of yellow flowers.' Work your way through the colours until all the children are seated. Collect the pictures from the children so they aren't distracted by them as you tell the story. When you have finished singing, praying and telling the Bible story, you could hand the pictures out again and see if the children can spot who has matching colours.

As you wait for the parents, give the children their paintings and their playdough.

Playdough – a basic recipe

1 cup of salt
2 cups of flour
2 tablespoons cooking oil or baby oil
2 teaspoons cream of tartar
2 cups of water
a few drops of food colouring

Mix all the ingredients in a saucepan. Cook over a medium heat, stirring continuously. The mixture will form a consistency similar to scrambled eggs and will start to come away from the side of the pan. A lump will form. Remove from heat, allow to cool and knead on a clean surface. Store in an airtight box or polythene bag. Keep in a cool place.

Recipe reproduced with permission of the Pre-school Learning Alliance, Rugby Branch.

JESUS IS OUR FRIEND — WEEK 3

Take Home!

JESUS TEACHES THE PEOPLE
(MATTHEW 6:25-34; LUKE 12:22-31)

Aim
To help the children understand that Jesus was special; that he taught the people about God's love.

Bible verses
Jesus taught people about God. (Matthew 5:1-2)
Jesus said, 'God knows the things you need.' (Luke 12:30)
Jesus told the people to love God more than anything else. (Matthew 6:33)

The story
Lots of people were with Jesus. They were asking him questions about money. Jesus wanted to teach them about God's love.

He said, 'Look at the birds in the sky. They find food to eat each day. But they don't worry about putting some away in a cupboard for another day. God takes care of them. You are more important to him than the birds.

'Look at the flowers. They don't go to a shop to buy clothes. They don't worry about what they look like. But they are beautiful - with so many different colours!

'If God takes such good care of the birds and flowers, he will certainly take care of you. He loves you very much.

'Don't worry about what you will eat and what you will wear. God knows what you need. The most important thing is to love him.'

Jesus taught the people about God. He wanted them to know how much God loved them.

Activity suggestions

Look at seed catalogues or gardening magazines together
Most shops that sell seeds would have small catalogues available. Even with a young baby you can look at the pictures and talk about the different colours and kinds of flowers. If your child is old enough, you may want to cut out some of the pictures to make a collage. As you enjoy the pictures together, tell your child about Jesus teaching the people.

Look at Bible verses with your child
Use whatever paper or card is available to you to make some bookmarks. Write one of today's verses on each one, and one or two from the other weeks in this unit on others. (If you haven't saved your Take Home! papers, your child's helper should be able to provide them for you.) Place the bookmarks at the correct reference in your Bible. As you sit with your child, say 'The Bible says...' and read a verse to them. You can do this even with a very young baby. If your child is older, they may want to help you decorate the bookmarks and choose which ones to read.

BIBLE STUFF

Jesus is our Friend   Week 4

PEOPLE SING TO JESUS (MATTHEW 21:1-11, LUKE 19:28-40)

Aim To help the children understand that Jesus was special; that many people were glad that Jesus had come.

Preparation

The story of Jesus' entry into Jerusalem has a depth of meaning for adults. But with the children, we shall simply take it at face value. Whatever their motives, there were many people in the crowd that day who were glad to see Jesus. As they sang to him, some of the people did not really understand what was happening. But others, with the eyes of faith, realized who Jesus was, and sang their songs of worship to him. The happy party atmosphere of that occasion is something we want to convey to the children today.

Jesus had no illusions about what was happening. He knew why he had come to Jerusalem. He knew that the time of his death was near. But he used the triumphal entry to make a dramatic statement about who he was.

Throughout his ministry, Jesus had claimed to be the One sent from God. The people were thrilled with the miraculous healings, and they marvelled at his teaching. But they still thought that the Messiah would come as a conquering king to save them from Roman rule.

So when Jesus came into Jerusalem on a donkey, they shouted 'Hosanna!', which means 'Save us now!' The donkey was not a humble beast as it is today. It was one of the animals associated with kings. The horse was the animal kings rode for war. The donkey was a symbol of coming in peace.

Seeing Jesus on a donkey made the people think of a king. But they seemed to miss the point he was making. He wasn't a king who would triumph by force - his was a kingdom of peace and love.

That is a very powerful statement for today's world, where so many people seem to think that they can get what they want by force or by war. The battle cry of the army of God is love. May God help us this week to win battles by love and peace.

As we worship this week, may we feel the joy and celebration that the throng felt on that day. But don't let it be just a case of joining the crowd. Let's pray that our worship will be rich on a personal level. May we be overflowing with praise as we know, ever deeper, the love and peace that King Jesus gives.

'Lord, as I worship you in private and in public this week, please help me to know a new release of joy and celebration. Thank you for being my Saviour. Amen.'

Story Time

Bible verses
Lots of people sang to Jesus as he went into Jerusalem. (Luke 19:37)
Jesus rode a donkey into Jerusalem. (Matthew 21:7)
The children were singing to Jesus in the church. (Matthew 21:15)

Week 4

Birth - 2s

Jesus was going to Jerusalem. Lots of other people were going there, too.

Jesus' helpers went to get a donkey for Jesus to ride. The people going along the road began to sing to him. They waved branches from the trees. They spread their coats on the ground to make a carpet for Jesus to ride on.

As they came into Jerusalem it was like a great big party. The people were happy because Jesus had made sick people well.

They sang songs to him and cheered for him.

Jesus loved the people very much. He wanted them to understand that he was God's Son.

3s - 5s

Jesus was on his way to Jerusalem. Lots of other people were going there too.

Jesus told his helpers where they would find a donkey for him to ride. They brought the donkey to Jesus. They spread their coats on its back for him to sit on.

As Jesus rode along on the donkey the people walking on the road began to sing to him. There were mummies and daddies and boys and girls. They waved branches from the trees as they sang. They spread their coats on the ground to make a carpet for Jesus to ride on.

As all the people came into Jerusalem it was like a great big party. They were singing and shouting. The people were happy because Jesus had made sick people well. They had heard him teach about God's love. They sang songs to him and cheered for him.

Jesus loved the people very much. He wanted them to understand that he was God's Son.

Teaching Activities

For adults, the happy Palm Sunday story is always linked with the sadness of Good Friday. Under fives don't make this connection yet. Although they may be able to say that 'Jesus died for our sins', it is unlikely that they understand what they are saying. So let's teach the story today with great joy. We want to communicate the happy atmosphere that should be present whenever we are worshipping Jesus.

Babies

Play a tape of lively music It shouldn't be too difficult to find a tape of joyful worship songs to play today. Choose one of your favourites; it will lift your spirit to God as it is played in the background.

Make bell rattles If you have a set of children's instruments you may already have some bells. Otherwise, you may be able to buy a few in a craft shop. You can sew them onto a wide piece of elastic, then make it into a wristband. A baby can hold it, or you can slide it onto his or her wrist. As babies jingle the bells you can tell them about how happy the people were as they sang to Jesus. (Supervise carefully so that the babies do not put bells into their mouths.)

BIBLE STUFF — God Loves Children/Jesus is our Friend

Week 4

Make a pull toy Obtain a shallow cardboard box and cover it with coloured paper. Punch a hole in one end of the box. Thread a 50 cm length of string through the hole and knot it on the inside of the box. Tie an empty cotton reel at the other end of the string, so that a baby may grasp it and pull the box along. Even a baby who is only sitting can pull the string to make the box move. Some babies may want to stack bricks or other toys in it, then tip them out. Sing to the babies about Jesus as they play.

Play with large bricks (older babies) Provide a set of large, plastic bricks (25 cm x 12 cm x 12 cm). Alternatively it is easy to make some. Save cardboard shoe boxes, cereal boxes, tissue boxes, etc. Stuff them with crumpled newspaper to increase their sturdiness. Cover them with plain paper. You will only need to make five or six for the babies, unless you have a very large group (more than ten).

Toddlers

Use large bricks with toddlers. If you are making them, you will need at least eight or ten bricks. If you have a very large group, the children will need to be helped to take turns. Play a tape of lively music as well. You may want to bring scarves, or some type of small flag or banner for the children to wave as they listen to the music. Tell them about the people singing to Jesus.

Other activities for toddlers include:
Look at seed catalogues The two older groups did this activity last week. As you look at the pictures of flowers and plants, sing songs about Jesus.

Water play Use an old baby bath or a washing-up bowl on a low table so that the children can stand to play. Cover the table and surrounding floor with newspaper or a plastic sheet. Cover the children's clothes with plastic aprons as well. Put a few plastic containers and a funnel or small sieve in the water. As the children enjoy the water, tell them the Bible verses for today.

2s - 3s

Put farm animals with the bricks It will be helpful if there is a donkey in the set of farm animals. Place them with the bricks. Tell the children about Jesus riding into Jerusalem on a donkey.

Make coloured paper collages Cover the working surface with old newspapers and provide aprons for the children. Cut out a variety of shapes from a selection of coloured papers. Provide glue, brushes and large sheets of white paper for background. Let the children select coloured paper shapes and stick them onto their background sheets. Try to let the children do as much of their own sticking as possible.

Work a 'fastening' puzzle If you are not handy with a needle and thread, ask someone else to make this puzzle for you. You will need a 30 cm square cushion. Sew several different types of fastenings to it: a zip; a large button and button hole; a Velcro fastening; a buckle; a popper; a toggle from a duffel coat. Place it with the other puzzles. Some children may need help at first, but then will want to try to do the different fastenings on their own. This puzzle will be a useful permanent addition to your resources. As you talk to children working this and other puzzles, tell them part of the Bible story. Similar puzzles are available commercially, but do try to make your own puzzle if possible. It will be different from any others that the children have seen.

Wash the dishes Put a few centimetres of warm soapy water in a washing-up bowl and provide several tea towels (for wiping dishes and mopping up spills). Let the children wash the dishes that you use in the home corner. You will need to cover their clothes with plastic aprons, and the floor with a plastic sheet or several layers of newspaper. Let the children take turns washing and wiping. Tell them, 'The Bible says, "Be kind". When you take turns you are being kind. You are doing what the Bible says.'

Week 4

3s - 5s

Bring a tape of joyful music today, as well as scarves, flags or banners for the children to wave and dance with. As they enjoy the music, tell them about the people singing to Jesus. Washing dishes in the home corner would also be an appropriate activity.

Some other ideas include:

Sort buttons This activity was used with 2s and 3s.

Colour with crayons Give the children chunky crayons in bright colours to do whatever drawing they want today. For a change, provide large sheets of paper cut in shapes other than squares and rectangles. As the children colour, tell them the Bible verses for today. Some of them may want you to write a Bible verse on their picture.

Look at nature pictures This activity has been suggested for both babies and toddlers in weeks 2 and 3. As children look at the pictures, help them to thank God for the world he has made.

Group Time

Songs you may want to use here are: 'Hosanna, hosanna' (Junior Praise, Marshall Pickering) and 'Hallelu, hallelu' (C & SSM 1).

2s - 3s

Sing to children as they tidy up the room for group time. For example, to the tune of 'Mulberry Bush', sing, 'It's time to put the toys away, the toys away, the toys away. It's time to put the toys away and you can be a helper.' As the children come to the circle, sing some activity songs or do several finger plays to settle them for the Bible story. After the usual group time activities, place six or seven of the farm animals on the floor. Let the children identify them. Ask them to close their eyes while you remove one of them. When they open their eyes, invite them to say which one is missing.

3s - 5s

You may want to start the group time by looking at the nature pictures. When you have finished talking about them with the children, put them out of sight so that you can tell the Bible story without any distractions.

At the end of the group time, you could put the music on again and let the children wave the scarves and flags. If you don't have enough for everyone, hand out the pictures they coloured during the session for them to wave to the music.

BIBLE STUFF

God Loves Children/Jesus is our Friend

JESUS IS OUR FRIEND — WEEK 4

Take Home!

PEOPLE SING TO JESUS
(MATTHEW 21:1-11, LUKE 19:28-40)

Aim
To help the children understand that Jesus was special; that many people were glad that Jesus had come.

Bible verses
Lots of people sang to Jesus as he went into Jerusalem. (Luke 19:37)
Jesus rode a donkey into Jerusalem. (Matthew 21:7)
The children were singing to Jesus in the church. (Matthew 21:15)

The story
Jesus was on his way to Jerusalem. Lots of other people were going there too.

Jesus told his helpers where they would find a donkey for him to ride. They brought the donkey to Jesus. They spread their coats on its back for him to sit on.

As Jesus rode along on the donkey the people walking on the road began to sing to him. There were mummies and daddies and boys and girls. They waved branches from the trees as they sang. They spread their coats on the ground to make a carpet for Jesus to ride on.

As all the people came into Jerusalem it was like a great big party. They were singing and shouting. The people were happy because Jesus had made sick people well. They had heard him teach about God's love. They sang songs to him and cheered for him.

Jesus loved the people very much. He wanted them to understand that he was God's Son.

Activity suggestions
Make a home-made pull toy for your baby or toddler
Cover a shallow cardboard box with plain paper. Punch a hole in one end and thread a piece of string through it. Tie a large knot on the inside end. Attach an empty cotton reel or something similar to the end your child will pull. They may enjoy putting small items, like bricks, into the box as they pull it. As your baby enjoys playing with the toy, tell them about the happy day when the people sang to Jesus.

Enjoy 'water-painting' with your child
On a bright day, take a container of water and a chunky child's paintbrush outside. Let your child paint the patio, the path or a wall (if it is a suitable surface) with water. As it dries, they can paint all over again. As you enjoy this activity together, tell your child this week's story, and talk about other stories about Jesus they have heard in recent weeks. If it rains all week(!) you could do this activity indoors by letting your child 'water-paint' a cardboard box.

BIBLE STUFF

Jesus is our Friend

week 5

FRIENDS SEE JESUS (LUKE 24)

Aim To help children understand that Easter is about Jesus; to associate Easter with joy.

Preparation

The story of Jesus' resurrection is well known to all Christians. In an academic sense, it's probably possible to reach a point where we think we know all that we need to know about it. But when it comes to our experience of it, we can never come to the end of knowing about the resurrection. Its power should be transforming our lives day by day. The fact that Jesus is alive is at the very centre of our faith. We don't worship a leader who is dead and gone. A living Lord is what makes Christianity unique. We worship one who chose to die on our behalf, then conquered death and now lives for ever.

Take some time to read the accounts of the resurrection given by Matthew, Mark, Luke and John. Find a quiet place and think about what you have read. Try to imagine what it must have been like for the women who first went to the tomb, for Mary when she realized it was Jesus who was speaking to her. What did the disciples think when the women came back with the story of the empty tomb and the angels? What would it have been like to be in the house on the evening of the first Easter day when Jesus was suddenly there?

As we meditate on the events of Easter, let's ask God to touch us again with the enormity of the significance of Jesus' death and resurrection. Our finite minds can never fully take in the amazing love that was demonstrated by God the Father in sacrificing his Son. But our hearts can be filled with worship and praise as we try to understand.

> 'Up from the grave he arose - with a mighty triumph o'er his foes!'
>
> 'Thine be the glory, risen, conquering Son,
> Endless is the victory thou o'er death hast won.'
>
> 'He's alive, he's alive, he has risen! Alleluia!'
>
> 'Thank you for the cross, the mighty cross,
> That God himself should die for such as us.
> And every day we're changed into his image more and more,
> For by the cross we've truly been transformed.
> And we're so amazed, and we give you praise,
> That you should save us at such a cost.
> And we're so amazed, and we give you praise,
> For the power of the cross.'
>
> Mark Altrogge
> © 1992 Integrity's Praise! Music / People of Destiny Int. PO Box 101, Eastbourne BN21 4SZ.
> All rights reserved. International copyright secured. Used by permission.

'Lord, please give me joy as I teach today. Give me patience with those children who are over-excited. Please, Father, give me wisdom to handle comments and questions about the Easter story. More than anything, Lord, may I please you with the worship of my life - as I sing, as I pray, and as I teach. In the name of my Redeemer, Jesus, Amen.'

Week 5

Story Time

Bible verses
Jesus' helpers were very happy when they saw him. (John 20:20)
An angel told some women that Jesus was alive. (Luke 24:6)

Birth - 2s
Jesus' friends and helpers were sad. Jesus had died. They would not see him again.

Early in the morning some women went to the place where Jesus was buried. A messenger from God told them, 'Do not be sad. Jesus is alive.'

Later that day, two people were walking home to their village. A man started to walk with them. It was Jesus, but they didn't know it was him.

When they got to their house, they asked him to come in for some food. As they ate some bread, they suddenly saw that it was Jesus who had been walking with them.

The two friends were so happy that Jesus was alive. They ran to tell Jesus' other friends and helpers.

3s - 5s
Jesus' friends and helpers were sad. Jesus had died. They would not see him again.

Early in the morning some women went to the place where Jesus was buried. A messenger from God told them, 'Do not be sad. Jesus is alive.' The women rushed to tell Jesus' other friends what they had seen.

Later that day, two people were walking home to their village. A man started to walk with them. It was Jesus, but they didn't know it was him.

When they got to their house, they asked him to come in for some food. As they ate some bread, they suddenly saw that it was Jesus who had been walking with them.

The two friends were so happy that Jesus was alive. They ran to tell Jesus' other friends and helpers. As they were telling what had happened, they all looked and saw Jesus. He was there with them.

Jesus helped his friends to understand what had happened to him. Jesus wanted them to tell everyone the good news that he loves people.

The friends were very happy to see Jesus.

Teaching Activities

Today, we want the children to know that Easter is about Jesus. It is a happy time because Jesus loves us, and we can love him too.

The details of Jesus' death and resurrection are beyond the understanding of most under fives. You will notice in the story that the emphasis is more on the happiness of Jesus' friends that they could see him again. Some children will have been told the whole Easter story. They may even tell you that 'Jesus died and rose again'. But they may not know what that means. They can repeat what they have heard without understanding it. We will need great wisdom to teach today. We don't want to tell children more than they can handle. Yet we want to communicate the tremendous joy of Easter.

Week 5

Babies

Play a tape of joyful worship songs You may want to bring some scarves or flags to wave as you play the music for the babies today. Even tiny babies will follow the movement with their eyes. As you cuddle and play with the babies, tell them a sentence or two of the story. Say things like, 'I am so glad to know that Jesus loves me. Jesus loves you, too, Emma.'

Look at pictures in gardening catalogues Select colourful pictures of flowers to show to babies. Let older babies handle the catalogues: it probably doesn't matter if the pages get torn, but you don't want babies to think that all books are for tearing. As you look at pictures of flowers, thank God for the things he has made. Say 'thank you' to God that Jesus loves us.

Play with a beach ball Bring a brightly coloured beach ball for babies to play with. You can throw it gently in the air for younger babies to watch. Older babies will want to roll or throw it themselves.

Toddlers

Paint with a pastel shade Add red, blue or green to white paint to make a pastel shade. Give the children chunky brushes and let them paint on large pieces of paper. Provide painting aprons.

2s - 3s

Make Easter cards Fold coloured paper in half to make cards. Let the children have washable felt tips and sticky shapes to decorate their cards. (You can purchase sticky shapes fairly cheaply. Try to get ones that are abstract shapes, rather than pictures.) Write 'Jesus loves us. Happy Easter!' on the inside of each card. Be ready to do any extra writing for those children who wish their cards to be addressed to a particular friend or relative.

3s - 5s

Make Easter cards Fold a sheet of paper in half. Let the children paint on the front with pastel shades. Use cotton buds instead of brushes. Only make a small amount of paint, and provide pale green, blue, pink and yellow. The children can dot with the cotton buds, or use them like brushes. Before they paint on the front, ask them who the card is for so that you can write an appropriate greeting on the inside. Some of the children will want to sign their own name.

It might be good to have one or two other ideas ready if children need extra stimulation - perhaps a floor puzzle, a different set of bricks or some nice picture books. Keep them out of sight and bring them out if you need them.

BIBLE STUFF

Week 5

Celebrate Easter!

You may be teaching this lesson on a Sunday other than Easter. If you want to run it as a normal session, you will need more activities for toddlers and 2s - 5s than are suggested. Look back through the previous four weeks and pick up any ideas you did not use. Or repeat one or two that were popular. Children often enjoy doing an activity again.

If, however, you want to try something different, here are some alternatives. They will be noisy and messy, but they should also be good fun as we communicate the joy of Easter. (NB These activities are not the kind you can do every week! All of them require extra supervision and help. Parents will need advance warning so that they can dress their child suitably or let you know of any allergies.)

Celebrate spring Because we celebrate Easter in the spring, things are starting to grow, and baby animals are born. Have a 'nature' day. Bring twigs from trees or bushes that are in bud, and spring flowers such as daffodils, tulips or hyacinths.

Check within your church, school and neighbourhood. Does anyone have a puppy, kitten, baby rabbit, chicks or ducklings? If you live in a farming area, you could be even more adventurous with a lamb or kid! The practicalities of this will depend on your numbers, facilities and timing. Enjoy God's created world with the children.

Have a tea party Bring snacks suitable for the age group you are working with. Jam sandwiches (cut into small squares or triangles), raisins, seedless grapes, pieces of banana or peeled apple, small crackers and bites of cheese would all be appropriate. Steer away from crisps, sweets, and sugary items. They are messy, and not really necessary!

Serve squash in beakers with lids for toddlers. For older under fives, just put a small amount in their cup. They can come back for more, and it makes less mess if they spill!

You may want to play a few simple games like Follow My Leader, blowing bubbles or keeping balloons in the air.

Paint handprints or footprints Make up paint in two or three colours. Add a few drops of washing-up liquid so the paint will wash off more easily. Provide a strong piece of paper for each child and let them choose a colour of paint. Depending on your facilities for washing, let them make handprints or footprints.

When a child has finished, write on their paper 'Sarah's hands' or 'Luke's feet' as appropriate, and the date. Because children will need to take turns, make sure you have other things for them to do and an adult to supervise while they are waiting or after they have had their turn.

JESUS IS OUR FRIEND — WEEK 5

Take Home!

FRIENDS SEE JESUS
(LUKE 24)

Aim
To help children understand that Easter is about Jesus; to associate Easter with joy.

Bible verses
Jesus' helpers were very happy when they saw him. (John 20:20)
An angel told some women that Jesus was alive. (Luke 24:6)

The story
Jesus' friends and helpers were sad. Jesus had died. They would not see him again.

Early in the morning some women went to the place where Jesus was buried. A messenger from God told them, 'Do not be sad. Jesus is alive.' The women rushed to tell Jesus' other friends what they had seen.

Later that day, two people were walking home to their village. A man started to walk with them. It was Jesus, but they didn't know it was him.

When they got to their house, they asked him to come in for some food. As they ate some bread, they suddenly saw that it was Jesus who had been walking with them.

The two friends were so happy that Jesus was alive. They ran to tell Jesus' other friends and helpers. As they were telling what had happened, they all looked and saw Jesus. He was there with them.

Jesus helped his friends to understand what had happened to him. Jesus wanted them to tell everyone the good news that he loves people.

The friends were very happy to see Jesus.

Activity suggestions
Do something practical for someone in your neighbourhood
Explain to your child that we can help other people to know that Jesus loves them by helping them and caring for them. Suggest a practical way you might do this - take some flowers to someone, take a cake or biscuits, help a neighbour with housework, shopping or gardening. Perhaps your child will want to make their own simple Easter card for the person. Let your child decorate the front of the card, then print a simple message inside, such as 'Jesus loves you. Happy Easter!'

(If your child is a baby or young toddler, you can still do this, explaining it simply. Children learn by imitation: if they grow up seeing their family sharing Jesus' love, they will learn to do it, too.)

BIBLE STUFF